4 $\frac{25}{N}$ AC

Structuralism and Christianity

DUQUESNE STUDIES

Theological Series

11

STRUCTURALISM AND CHRISTIANITY

By

Günther Schiwy

Duquesne University Press, Pittsburgh, Pa.

Editions E. Nauwelaerts, Louvain

DUQUESNE STUDIES

Theological Series

Henry J. Koren, S.T.D., Editor

Translated from the German edition
STRUKTURALISMUS UND CHRISTENTUM by Gunther Schiwy
Published by Herder KG, Freiburg
Copyright 1969 by Herder KG, Freiburg

Copyright, 1971 by Duquesne University

First Printing

Library of Congress catalog card number: 75-176036

ISBN-0-8207-0138-6

PRINTED IN THE UNITED STATES OF AMERICA

CONTENTS

TRANSLATOR'S PREFACE

THIS BOOK has been translated from the original German edition by the undersigned. The author's references and quotations from works in German editions have been replaced, wherever possible, by references to the English editions of these works or their original texts. Indexes have been added for the convenience of the reader.

The translator wishes to thank Dr. James Erpenbeck for his kind assistance in making the translation more readable.

Henry J. Koren

AUTHOR'S PREFACE

CHRISTIANITY has gotten into a crisis which continues unabated both within and without the Catholic Church. This crisis has many causes. One of them undoubtedly is the appearance of competing world-views. These are all the more dangerous today because they present themselves with scientific pretensions. For modern "believers" demand, though not always explicitly, that a world-view satisfy scientific requirements. It is considered satisfactory, however, if a world-view can convincingly show why its tenets escape scientific verification. But at least this proof must be presented on a scientific level.

First to be named among the world-views which seriously compete with Christianity is Marxism. Neo-Marxism, above all, which, beyond communist ideologies, reflects upon the scientific foundation of Marxism, is becoming more and more a challenge that the Christian must take seriously. But this is not our topic here. Rather, we wish to draw attention to structuralism. Starting from France, structuralism for the past few years has been raising questions for the scientific and philosophical thinking of our time. Whether it wants or not, structuralism is becoming a world-view which competes with Marxism as well as Christianity.

The rapid rise of structuralism finds a partial explanation in the fact that for some time now orthodox Marxism and orthodox Christianity have been showing symptoms of a certain tiredness. Both groups try to overcome these symptoms by movements of radical change—such as Vatican Council II and Neo-Marxism—but their results are not yet certain. In this way many people find themselves in a vacuum as far as their world-view is concerned. In this vacuum structuralism appears as a welcome explanation not only for the failure of Christianity and Marxism but for the problems of mankind in general.

Structuralism, however, is not merely attractive to people whose world-view has lost its moorings. It definitely also has the power to gain followers from among the "believers" in Marxism as well as in Christianity because of its very modern scientific character. It takes up and vigorously pursues theoretical questions which today in the sciences of nature and of man indicate the most progressive positions, such as analysis of language, critique of ideology, the objectification, functionalization and decentralization of man, and sociologization. By doing this, structuralism exercises a profound power of attraction on young intellectuals, from which they can only escape with great effort through counter-watchwords with a Marxist or a Christian coloring, such as hermeneutics, political involvement, humanization, moral renewal and re-subjectification.

As with respect to Marxism, so also in reference to structuralism, the issue for Christianity cannot be simply to reject this scientific movement with its philosophy of life. To the extent that the scientific statements of structuralism are valid, the Christian has the duty to accept them, even if in the process his own ideas and modes of conduct, which hitherto he had accepted as beyond discussion from a Christian standpoint, are corrected. For, after all, the Christian wishes to be faithful to reality. That's why he is fundamentally well-disposed toward science and scholarship and grateful for every new achievement of knowledge, even when it replaced trusted prejudices by true judgments. A world-view can be implied in such scientific achievements or it can be explicitly proposed as something which is beyond scientific verification and which, in final analysis, constitutes a "system of faith." The Christian will not hesitate to let his own faith be challenged by it; he will compare the inner temper of any world-view with that of his own; and he will measure both again by his own experience and even more by the experience of all mankind. And then he will, renewed, confirm the option he has made as a Christian or revoke his option.

The confrontation with such contemporary movements which are both scientific and a philosophy of life would demand too much of the solitary individual. That's why their challenge should be taken up by all of Christianity and not left to the individual. The intellectual elite of Christianity in particular is challenged to take a stand with respect to both Neo-Marxism and structuralism. In our case it is structuralism which, above all, addresses to theology as a science, questions that cannot be disregarded with impunity. These questions can all the more easily be taken into account because most structuralists have no intention of making any direct attacks on Christianity. This is not always the case among Marxists, for reasons derived from the history of Marxist development. And it is possible that taking up the structuralistic attitude of questioning will also help theology attain again the degree of scientific competence to which it lays claim but which it cannot always achieve because it has not been able to keep pace with the development of the sciences.

It is our intention to formulate here on the basis of a first personal encounter with structuralism a few questions and problems with which, in our opinion, it challenges Christianity. The sooner Christian thought enters into a discussion of these problems with the kind of openness that should be a honor to a Christian, the sooner also both Christianity and structuralism can profit therefrom. For structuralism itself also needs our challenge and our criticism. It is only by way of such a critical discussion that mankind comes closer to the truth which it needs and for which it still continues to look, although this truth, I believe, is present in our midst.

Günther Schiwy

Chapter One

A SHORT HISTORY OF STRUCTURALISM

LET US BEGIN by sketching in a few words the history of the movement known as "structuralism." After that, we can raise the questions which structuralism puts to Christianity and therein we will see what structuralism is.

Claude Lévi-Strauss, who was born in 1908 in Brussels, is considered to be the Father of structuralism. A French ethnologist with a sociological orientation, he published in 1949 his work *Les structures élémentaires de la parenté* (English edition forthcoming). He was the first ethnologist who consistently "took the structural character of social phenomena . . . seriously and serenely drew all the consequences from it."[1]

1. *Lévi-Strauss Against Sartre*

In 1962 Lévi-Strauss published his work *La Pensée sauvage* (English edition forthcoming), which brought the structuralistic way of thinking closer to a wider public. It also indicated the consequences of structuralism for our world-view since in the

---

1. Jean Pouillon, *Les Temps modernes*, July 1956, p. 158. Lévi-Strauss has appropriated this judgment as his program. Cf. his *Structural Anthropology*, New York, 1963, Preface, p. 1.

last chapter Lévi-Strauss argues against Sartre and addresses to him the following reproach:

> One who begins by establishing himself in the alleged evidence of the *I* no longer has any chance of escape. The knowledge of man sometimes seems easier to attain to people who let themselves be caught in the trap of personal identity. But they thereby lock the door to knowledge of man: all ethnographic research has its starting point in written or unavowed "confessions." As a matter of fact, Sartre does become the prisoner of his *cogito*. Descartes' *cogito* still allowed access to the universal, albeit only on condition that it remain psychological and individual. But by sociologizing the *cogito*, Sartre merely changes the prison. For him henceforth the groups and epoch of every subject replaces timeless consciousness. Besides, Sartre's outlook on the world and on man shows that narrowness by which traditionally closed societies are recognized. The persistence with which he, bravely appealing to arbitrary contrasts between primitive and civilized man, posits a distinction reflects in a barely differentiated form the fundamental opposition which he postulates between the *I* and the other. Yet this opposition is formulated in Sartre's work in a way that hardly differs from that of a Melanesian savage; and his analysis of the "practico-inert" simply restores the language of animism. Descartes, who wanted to lay the foundation for a physics, cut man off from society. Sartre, who wants to lay the basis for an anthropology, cuts his society off from other societies.[2]

The tone and the topic of this passage are such that since then peace has not yet returned to Paris.

To this must be added a feud between the structuralists and the traditionalists which broke out in 1965-66 in the critique of literature and in which Roland Barthes and Raymond Picard

---

2. *La pensée sauvage*, Plon, Paris, n.d., pp. 329 f.

were the leading figures.[3] Structuralism is essentially "at home" in linguistics; although one cannot say that linguistics has given birth to modern structuralism, it has given it its foundations. But the above-mentioned feud made it perfectly clear that from linguistics, by way of ethnology, sociology and psychology, had now also penetrated into literature.

2. Pessimism of Culture

How fashionable "structuralism" thereafter became is proved also by Lévi-Strauss's autobiography, *Tristes tropiques*. First published in 1955, it appeared as a paperback in 1965. It soon became a bestseller and was praised as a "classic" work. The scientific method of structuralism became thereby a fashionable world-view, in which the public at large showed great interest. People who had previously been intoxicated by a vision of the future offered by a man like Teilhard de Chardin, now could read an opposing view written by a man who had led no less an adventurous life dedicated to the exact sciences: "What indeed have I learned from the masters to whom I have listened, from the philosophers whom I have read, from the societies which I have visited, or even from the science of which the West is so proud? What else have I learned but fragments which, when put together, constitute the meditation of the wise man at the foot of the tree? Any attempt to understand disturbs the object of our attention in favor of one whose nature is different. This one, again, demands a new effort which, in its turn, disturbs it

---

3. R. Picard, *Nouvelle critique ou nouvelle imposture*, Paris, 1965; R. Barthes, *Critique et vérité*, Paris, 1966.

in favor of a third, a fourth, a fifth, until at last we find the approach to the only lasting present, the one in which the difference between meaning and the absence of meaning disappears, the one from which we have started" (p. 446).

3. The End of Humanism?

The winter semester of 1966-67 produced a fundamental discussion of structuralism in all disciplines. It was initiated by the appearance of important works by or about structuralists. Lévi-Strauss published the second volume of his research into the myths of primitives;[4] the Communist Louis Althusser and his colleagues despite Party opposition attempted to read Marx structuralistically;[5] the leader of the French Freudians Jacques Lacan published almost one thousand pages of collected essays;[6] and the young Michel Foucault revealed himself as the most radical representative of the structuralistic world-view in his work, *Les mots et les choses*. This book became the philosophical bestseller of the season although—or rather precisely because—its author had the cheek to declare in an interview:

The "I" is destroyed—think only of modern literature—the issue now is to discover the "there is." There is an "impersonal they" (*on*). In a certain sense this means a return to the standpoint of the seventeenth century, with this difference, however: we do not put man in the place of God but we start with anonymous thinking, knowledge

---

4. The entire book, entitled *Mythologiques*, contains *Le crue et le cuit* (Paris, 1964), *Du miel au cendre* (Paris, 1966), *L'origine des manières de table* (Paris, 1968).

5. *Pour Marx*, Paris, 1965; *Lire le Capital*, 2 vols., Paris, 1966.

6. *Ecrits*, Paris, 1966.

without a subject, a theoretical [entity] without identity. . . . It can be said, I think, that humanism pretends to solve problems which it is not permitted to raise . . . , such as the relations of man with the world, the problem of reality, of artistic creation, happiness and all those hallucinations which don't at all deserve to be theoretical problems. . . . To save man, to re-discover man in man, etc., this means the end of all those garrulous theoretical and practical ventures which, for example, try to reconcile Marx and Teilhard de Chardin. For years now the sheer humanism of such ventures has condemned all intellectual efforts to sterility. It is our task finally to get rid of humanism. In this sense our work is a political work, insofar as all regimes of both East and West peddle their bad wares under the flag of humanism.[7]

4. *The New International?*

The argument about structuralism has not ceased since then. The events of May, 1968, in Paris may have interrupted it for a moment or let it fade into the background, but precisely the way in which the social system apparently emerged strengthened from the confusion seems to have vindicated the structuralists.[8] At any rate, the experts unanimously give a negative answer to the question whether the May movement has killed structuralism.[9] One can even be of the opinion that, alongside Neo-Marxism, structuralism constitutes a kind of second "International."[10] It is significant in this respect that it has also made

---

7. *La Quinzaine littéraire*, no. 5, 1966.

8. Cf. Schiwy, "Im Zeichen der linken Frustration?," *Der französische Strukturalismus*, Reinbek, 1969, pp. 24-28.

9. "Le Structuralisme, a-t-il été tué par le mouvement de mai?" *Le Monde*, Nov. 30, 1968.

10. Schiwy, "Die neue Internationale," *op. cit.*, pp. 29-35.

its entrance into German universities, as is evident from the first publications of seminar proceedings:

> What I found fascinating is the bond which structuralism lays between theory and method. While the arguments between dialecticians and neo-positivists in Germany slowly but surely turned around in a circle from which the purely theoretical discussion could no longer escape, the discussion here took place on a more fundamental level. Sociology was, in a way, put into question and issued a challenge which to me appeared to be fundamental. Not without reason has it been said that what is at stake in the controversy between structuralism, existentialism and Marxism is a coming to grips with the aims envisioned by the modern age, that is, with the possibilities of development of modern society.[11]

This quotation speaks of structuralism's fundamental challenge to sociology and the issue of the future of our society. We need only to substitute Christianity for sociology to return to the topic of our book. We will now directly take up this topic without any further details about structuralism as such.

_____

11. Urs Jaeggi, *Ordnung und Chaos; Strukturalismus als Methode und Mode*, Frankfurt a.m., 1968, p. 7.

Chapter Two

THE STRUCTURELL AND THE STRUCTURAL

EVEN IN THE WORKS by and about structuralists the distinction between the structurell and the structural is not always perceived, or at least expressed, with sufficient clarity. Nevertheless, we intend to make this distinction the starting point of our discussion, for this distinction is fundamental if one wishes to show how French structuralism differs from other sciences which also speak of "structure."

For example, Eduard Spranger presents the following definition in reference to "structural psychology": "An edifice of reality has an articulate structure if it is in a whole in which each part and each partial function performs a task that is important for the whole, and this in such a way that the structure and task of each part in its turn can be understood in terms of the whole."[1] In this definition the term "structure" refers to the "objective reality" of the soul, the molecule, society, a landscape, etc.; briefly put, it refers to the *structurell*.

If, on the other hand, a structuralist belonging to the movement discussed here speaks of structure, he does not directly refer to the "objective reality" of things, but to the models

---

1. *Psychologie des Jugendalters*, Heidelberg, 19th ed., 1949, p. 8.

man has made of them for himself, the systems of interpretation and complexes of meaning in which man tries to grasp things in order to use and understand them. Briefly put, the structuralist refers to the *structural*. That's why, speaking about "social structure," Lévi-Strauss can say:

> The term "social structure" has nothing to do with empirical reality but with models which are built up after it. This should help one to clarify the difference between two concepts which are so close to each other that they often have been confused, namely, *social structure* and *social relation*s. . . . *Social relations* consist of the raw material out of which the models making up the *social structure* are built. . . . Then the question becomes that of ascertaining what kind of models deserves the name "structure."[2]

This quotation shows that the structural, the model of "objective reality," as a rule takes its starting point in this "reality," using it as raw material, and that the structural also aims at the "objectively real." It may and often does go further to make the claims that only the structural properly represents "objective reality." The structural—like "sound reason"—wishes to bring to light a certain truth about the structurell.

Nevertheless, one can abstract from this relationship between the object and its representation to concentrate one's attention solely on investigating how man proceeds when he creates such models, how such models are constituted, what kind of structure they have. This is precisely what French structuralism does. It is a science of the structural and not of the structurell; it does not ask—at least, not in the first instance—how the struc-

---

2. "Social Structure," in *Anthropology Today*, ed. by Sol. Tax, University of Chicago Press, 1962, p. 322.

tural is related to the structurell or whether the structure of the model agrees more or less with the structure of its object. That the structurell exists, that it also has a structure and that there is a relationship between the structural and the structurell—all this structuralism as a science does not deny; it merely abstracts from these concerns.

For structuralism thinks that the structural, on its part, is such an important "objective reality" for man that it is worth while making it the exclusive object of a science. The knowledge achieved by this science, it holds, will at the same time be knowledge about man. For man is clearly characterized by this that he constantly devises models of reality in order to dominate and understand it better. Conceived in this way, structuralism would have an important contribution to make to that science of man which today is known by the collective title of anthropology.

1. *Christianity as Model and Christian Reality*

How is this structuralistic distinction between the structural and the structurell and the limitation of structuralism to the investigation of the structural a challenge to contemporary Christianity? Christianity zealously tries to bring man closer to "objective reality" and offers him an all-encompassing model of the world—God included. But in its zeal it runs the risk of disregarding, dismissing as self-evident, or even simply forgetting that the Christian model, by the mere fact of being "Christian," does not cease to be a "model" and does not begin to replace "objective reality" itself. This danger exists for the

Christian especially because he is convinced that his model of the world corresponds to reality. Thus he is greatly tempted to identify the model with reality, instead of "merely" saying: our model is true to reality in what it ultimately wishes to say about reality, and on condition that it be properly understood.

The Christian must, for the sake of reality, take the distinction between the structural and the structurell more seriously again than he has hitherto done; he must also recall that, according to Christian conviction, man finds his salvation by being in harmony with reality, and not simply by having a model of the world which is in harmony with reality. Precisely when he does this, the Christian will ask himself the following questions. Is it possible for man to be in contact with reality and to act toward reality as he ought to without having a theoretical model which conforms with reality? Is it perhaps even possible to act in a practically correct way while having a theoretically false model? If this is true or at least cannot be excluded, then the Christian will take it into account that he may meet human beings with whom one can practically live and work together, without reaching agreement in the theoretical model. The Christian will then also be cautious in maintaining that the other's salvation always depends on his acceptance of the Christian model. Yet, he will insist that one is confessionally a Christian only when one knows and accepts the Christian model of reality and tries to see and live reality accordingly.

2. *Ideological Transgressions*

Structuralism as a science abstracts, we said, from the question how the models of reality which man fashions for himself are related to this reality itself, whether they more or less do justice to it. But transgressions of this restriction occur all the time among structuralists, and they tend toward a relativism which the Christian does not share. For example, Lévi-Strauss writes:

> Neither psychology nor metaphysics nor art can offer me a refuge, for henceforth they have become myths answerable even from within to a new kind of sociology, which will arise one day and not treat them more kindly than the old sociology. The I is not merely hateful; there is not even room for it between a we and a nothing. And when I finally decide in favor of this we—although this is a matter of mere pretense—then I do this because there remains no other possible choice in between pretense and nothing if I do not wish to destroy myself. But the act of choosing alone is enough for me to accept unconditionally my human condition. In this way I get rid of an intellectual pride, whose vanity I can measure by the vanity of its aim. At the same time, I am also ready to subordinate its idle pretensions to those objective demands needed for the liberation and redemption of the many people to whom the possibility of such a choice has always been denied.[3]

There is no absolute relativism and agnosticism in this quotation since Lévi-Strauss pretends to acknowledge "objective demands" of reality. But the content of these demands is this: all models explaining the world—from the old myths to the modern myths of the sciences—have led man astray insofar as they did not come to the realization that there is no other "objective knowledge" for man than that of the absolute meaninglessness of existence. The "relative truth" of all human projects of existence, according to Lévi-Strauss, consists in this that they are more or less successful attempts of man to cover up the horror of his meaningless existence.

In this way Lévi-Strauss assumes the position of a philosophi-

---

3. *Tristes tropiques*, p. 448.

cal world-view. While making use of the structuralistic distinction between the structurell and the structural, this world-view goes beyond structuralism as the science of the structural. It makes statements about the relationship of certain structural models to the structure of reality which are of a philosophical nature and which can no longer be established by means of the methods of structural analysis.

Roland Barthes is apparently more consistent when he describes the function of the poet and the writer in contrast to that of the literary critic in the following way:

> Every novelist and every poet, no matter what wrong turns literary theory may take, is considered to be a man who speaks about things and phenomena—even if they are purely imaginary—which lie outside language or precede language. The world exists and the writer uses language—that's literature.
>
> The object of critique, however, is entirely different. The critique of literature is not concerned with the world but with the language statements made by other individuals. It is, therefore, a statement about a statement; consequently, a *secondary* language. As logicians would express it, it is a *meta-language* referring to a primary or object-language. . . . Accordingly, if literary critique is nothing but a meta-language, its task cannot at all consist in the discovery of truths but at most in that of validities. A language in itself is neither true nor false, but rather valid or invalid. "Valid" here means that it must build a coherent system of signs. And the rules governing a language of literature do not refer to the agreement of this language with reality (no matter what the realistic school may demand), but only to the internal obedience to the system of signs decided upon by the author.[4]

---

4. "Die Literaturkritik als Metasprache," *Kritiker unserer Zeit*, ed. by Hans Mayer, Pfullingen, 1967, pp. 23 f.

This task which Roland Barthes assigns to literary critique remains entirely within the framework of the structuralism which he (and we) have in mind. The question, however, why the critique has only this task and not also that of verifying to what extent the writer has remained faithful to reality can no longer be decided within the context of structuralism. It is a philosophical question which must be answered within the framework of a philosophical sociology of literature with the aid of aesthetic and sociological criteria.

We hope the preceding examples have shown the point at which the Christian challenges the structuralist. The latter may not unwittingly pass from statements about the structural, about which he can speak with competence and for which he must develop methods, to statements about the structurell. If he makes such statements anyhow, he makes them in the name of other sciences, of philosophy, theology or a personal "confession of faith." Otherwise he practically abolishes the distinction between the structurell and the structural, for the introduction of which the Christian owes him a debt of gratitude.

Chapter Three

LANGUAGE AND SPEECH

A CLOSER ANALYSIS of the models which mankind in the course of time has created in order to explain and dominate the world shows that, as a rule, these models either directly make use of language or would have been impossible without language. Even language itself reveals itself as a model of the world, the primordial model, the first and fundamental project of the world, the model in which everyone who speaks lives.

1. *Humboldt, de Saussure, Lévi-Strauss*

This idea is not new. As early as the beginning of the nineteenth century, Wilhelm von Humboldt wrote that the external conception of language as a system of signs for "objects already perceived in themselves" is clearly contradicted by the fact that "the entire way of subjective perception of objects necessarily" permeates the "formation and usage of language." The language with which one describes something contains also the describer's individual world-view, just as "also a similar subjectivity influences the language in the same nation." In this context Humboldt also wrote his famous statement: "By the same act in which man "spins" language out of himself he also envelops himself in his web; and every language draws around the people who listen to it a circle from which escape is only possible by passing over into the circle of another language." The learning of a foreign language "must therefore be the acquisition of a new standpoint with respect to the previous way of viewing the world." This acquisition is never wholly successful because one "always more or less introduces one's own world-view and one's own view of language into the foreign language."[1]

In the science of language Ferdinand de Saussure is important for us. In the text of his lectures, posthumously published in 1916, he was first in consistently describing language as the most important interpretation model of the world and making this idea the principle of his scientific work. He thereby laid the foundation for structural philology, which in its turn became the foundation of the modern structuralism with which we are concerned here.

Language, de Saussure pointed out, is a system of signs that express ideas. It can therefore be compared to a system of writing, the alphabet of deaf-mutes, symbolic rites, military signals, etc. But language is the most important of all these systems. De Saussure then proceeded to plan the science of semiology, to which the structuralism with which we are concerned here belongs and to which he had already given a powerful impetus.

One can envision, so de Saussure wrote, *a science which investigates the life of signs within society*, a science which I

---

1. "Einleitung in die Kawi-Sprache," *Werke*, vol. 7, Berliner Akademie, 1889 ff., pp. 59 f.

will call *semiology* (from the Greek *semeion*, sign). This science would teach us what constitutes signs and what laws govern them. Linguistics, he adds, is only a part of this general science. The laws discovered by semiology will be applicable to linguistics and the latter will be concerned with a well-defined area in the totality of the anthropological data. The reason why this science of semiology has not yet been recognized as an autonomous science having, like any other, its own object, is that linguists have been moving in circles. On the one hand, nothing is as appropriate as language for understanding the semiological problem; on the other hand, to raise this problem correctly, language must be studied in itself. But hitherto language has nearly always been studied in connection with something else, from other standpoints. So far de Saussure.[2]

Lévi-Strauss has given us an example of how in modern structuralism the language model serves to make it possible to see and explain in detail other phenomena of our life together as systems of signs. He did this when he succeeded in reducing the complex rules of marriage in primitive cultures to a uniform system of relations. Speaking of this he says:

> These results have only been achieved by treating marriage regulations and kinship systems as a kind of language, a set of processes permitting the establishment, between individuals and groups, of a certain type of communication. That the mediating factor, in this case, should be the *women of the group*, who are *circulated* between clans, lineages, or families, in place of the *words of the group*, which are *circulated* between individuals, does not at all change the fact that the essential aspect of the phenomenon is identical in both cases. . . .

2. *Course in General Linguistics*, Philosophical Library, New York, 1959, p. 16.

For marriage regulations, in relation to language, represent a complex much more rough and archaic than the latter. It is generally recognized that words are signs: but poets are practically the only ones who know that words have also been values. As against this, women are held by the social group to be values of the most essential kind, though we have difficulty in understanding how these values become integrated in systems endowed with a significant function. . . . The question may be raised whether the different aspects of social life (including even art and religion) can not only be studied by the methods, and with the help of concepts similar to those employed by linguistics, but also whether they do not constitute phenomena whose inmost nature is the same as that of language.[3]

2. *The Primordial Form of Revelation*

Language, then, is viewed as the fundamental model of the world, and one can show to what extent language can also serve to discover and explain other systems of signs. The Christian who is confronted with all this will at once look upon it as an unexpected confirmation of fundamental Christian convictions, even if these convictions have sometimes been obscured by deviating practices for which subsequently verbal justifications were offered.

First of all, there is the high esteem which the word and language in general have always enjoyed in Christianity. The Gospel of St. John begins with the program-like sentence: "In the beginning was the word, and the word was with God, and the word was God. This was in the beginning with God. Everything was made by it, and nothing was made without it." In

---

3. Lévi-Strauss, "Language and the Analysis of Social Laws," *American Anthropologist*, vol. 53 (1951) pp. 159 f.

connection with structuralism this prologue raises the question: Shouldn't the Christian admit that structuralism is right? Isn't language for the Christian, on theological grounds, the primordial form of revelation, even as for the structuralist it is the primordial form of world-view and world-model? What would any other "sign from heaven"—such as the beauty of the world or its catastrophes, "wonderful events" and even the astounding deeds of a Jesus from Nazareth—be without language? What would it be if it were not interpreted, explained, signified by a word and thereby incorporated into an already existing system of meaning, a "world-view"?

The Christian understands at once in this context that the dispute among Christians about "word and sacrament" was not a battle about mere words and that it continues to retain its validity even today, at least as long as there is no realization of this idea: if there is a primordial sacrament, a sign, in which God must first of all speak to us if all further speaking in other signs is to be intelligible, then this primordial sacrament is the word in its system, language as a "world-view."

3. Christian Language Disputes

There exists also a "language dispute" within Christianity, particularly in the Catholic Church, as the recent experience in connection with the language of the liturgy shows. In structuralistic categories the substance of this language dispute also appears as thoroughly modern. The Church realized, if not always reflectively, then at least instinctively, that the abandonment of Latin as the universally obligatory language of worship and Church affairs would put into question the Catholic's common way of "looking at the world." Reversely, the tendency of the individual language groups to confess their faith in their native tongue is a legitimate expression of the fact that a faith cannot really become a people's own faith unless it is incorporated into this people's living way of looking at the world, and this means into their language.

For this reason a literal translation of the formulas of faith from one language into another is from the very outset a problematic procedure. The "translation" cannot be called successful unless it becomes fully assimilated. Such a complete assimilation will as a rule probably find verbal expression in a reformulation. There is no reason, then, to be surprised if the people in Rome have their troubles with the Dutch Catechism. But such difficulties should be resolved on a basis which puts neither the Romans nor the Dutch to shame. And if the Americans are looking for a catechism of their own, the Dutch Catechism cannot be more than a stimulus; the American catechism will either develop from the American language itself or there will not be any. There is, however, also a possibility that with the increasingly progressive assimilation of languages, the world-views also will become more unified; this would make translations from one language into another easier.

4. *Tradition and Dogma*

These considerations are important for Christianity, not only insofar as it wishes to be a world-wide community of faith but also because it possesses a great tradition and even considers itself the guardian of a unique tradition, viz., the life, death and resurrection of Jesus from Nazareth as the last word of God to the world. If we ask how such a tradition can be successful, and what means must be used less the tradition becomes falsified in being passed on from one generation to another, then Christendom's answer is the key-word "dogma."

The dogma is a verbal way of "fixing" something for the purpose of providing a valid formulation for a disputed or forgotten matter and keeping this matter in mind. Structuralistically there are no objections to such a procedure. But one should ask whether this "fixing" can legitimately mean that future generations and languages must profess their faith in this formulation as the only valid way of stating things. Doesn't such a rigid "fixing" mean that the matter, fastened to, and preserved in a particular language, is also by the same token condemned to death since this language will sooner or later cease to belong to the living systems of communication, at least as the language of a particular generation of a people speaking the same language? How can a dogma "fixed" in such a way ever become the living possession of a community of believers who, in the mean time, have begun to speak a different language?

Obviously, the issue cannot be to declare that the traditional earlier formulation of a dogma is not binding; that would indeed be "the end of traditional Christianity," that is to say, of a Christianity which conceives itself bound to matters which became known at an earlier age and were formulated in binding formulas that must be passed on. The issue is how the matters contained in such formulations can be made alive today. The answer of structuralism is: by letting them enter into today's language, without giving up the matter itself. This process must constantly be checked by referring to the traditional formulation of the dogma; and this would constitute the task of theology and the teaching office of the Church.

One can analogically apply to a suitable preaching of Christian dogmas what Roland Barthes describes as the task of contemporary literary criticism with respect to the poetry of the past:

> Its task consists solely in developing for itself a language in order that by this language's coherence and logic—in other words, through its systematics—the greatest possible quantity of Proust's language can be gathered or rather, in the mathematical sense of the term, "integrated," and this in exactly the same way as a logical equation examines the validity of a conclusion without assuming a standpoint with respect to the truth of the argument in question. Accordingly, one can say that the task of the critique is exclusively of a formal nature; and this is also the only guarantee for its universality. The aim of the critique is not to discover in the work or the author under consideration something "hidden," "profound" or even "mysterious," which has hitherto escaped notice.
>
> Besides, by what miracle could such a thing happen? Are we perchance more intelligent today than were our forebears? No, the aim of the critique is simply to act more or less like a good cabinet-maker who, adroitly groping, fits together two pieces of a complicated piece of furniture. The critique tries to adapt the language given to it by its own time, for instance, the language given by existentialism, Marxism or psychoanalysis, to that of the author, that is to say, to the formal system of logical rules which the author had developed in the conditions of his era.
>
> The "demonstration" of a particular literary critique has nothing to do with the "truth," for the critical statement—as also the logical statement—is always merely tautological. It ultimately consists of the "later" formulated observation—and one is fully aware of this "late-

ness," a point that is not without importance—that Racine is really Racine, that Proust is really Proust. No, the "proof" of a critique, if it exists at all, is not found in the ability to *dis*cover the work under consideration, but on the contrary to *cover* it in the best manner possible with our own language.[4]

5. *Language and the Bible*

The high esteem of Christianity for the word and dogma culminates in the role which the book of holy writ, the Bible, plays among Christians. True, it is not right, I think, to call Christianity a book religion, for Christianity is not primarily based on a book but on Jesus of Nazareth, who did not leave behind any book. Nevertheless, it remains true that Christianity would never have had such a fruitful history if the figure of Jesus Christ had not been written up in a book. Besides, he himself explicitly appealed to the Old Testament, the books of the Jewish religion to which he belonged by descent and without which he cannot be understood. For this reason these books of the Old Testament, together with the writings of the first Christian generations—the New Testament—constitute the documents to which the Christian appeals.

These Christian facts are easily understood from the standpoint of structuralism. The most perfect means at man's disposal for the expression of a world-view is language. Jesus, therefore, could not disregard this means if he did not wish to fall behind other revealers. Moreover, he had to remain in contact with a language developed in the course of millennia and to attempt

---

4. "Die Literaturkritik als Metasprache," in *Kritiker unserer Zeit*, ed. by Hans Meyer, pp. 24 f.

to express his "message" within the world-view which had already richly developed in this language. Otherwise he would not have been able to compete and would from the very start have been doomed to a subjectivistic sectarianism without prospects. For sectarianism begins with the presumption of individuals that they can create their own language out of nothing. But the few original points that they have to say cannot outweigh the fullness of what they give up by giving up the rich language of tradition.

6. *The Superior Power of Language*

In this context attention must also be paid to the fact that Jesus at first, like any man, was the "prisoner" of the language and the world-view in which he grew up and of which he made use. But by the very fact that man "uses" them, he shows that he is not wholly at the mercy of the system. The prophetic talent consists precisely in the ability to transcend the linguistic and conceptual categories of a system in a better than average way.

This is a truth which Christianity must defend against a structuralistic world-view which argues that man is totally at the mercy of the system, but is not able to justify its position through structural analysis. For example, Michel Foucault says:

> Lacan's importance is based on the fact that he has shown how the system of language—and not the subject—expresses itself throughout the words of the patient and the symptoms of his illness. Before every human existence, before every human thought, then, there is already a kind of knowing, a system, which we re-discover.

. . . What is this anonymous system without a subject, what is it that thinks? . . . One thinks within an anonymous and compelling system of thought, namely, that of an epoch and a language. This thinking and this language have their own laws of change. The task of today's philosophy and of all theoretical disciplines . . . consists in bringing to light again this thinking which precedes thinking, this system before any system. From it, our "free" thinking emerges and lights up for a moment. . . . In order to think the system, I would have to be compelled by a system-behind-the-system which I do not know and which will recede to the same extent as I will discover it and as it will disclose itself.[5]

In reply to this statement, Jean-Paul Sartre writes:

Transcendence, at least transcendence by man, is not wanted. This is a return to positivism, not a positivism of facts, but of signs: there are totalities, structured complexes constituting themselves through man; and man's only task is to decipher these. . . . [But, argues Sartre,] the essential point is not what people make of man, but *what man makes of what people have made of him*. What they have made of man are the structures, the complexes of meaning, explored by the human sciences. But what man makes that is history itself, the real transcendence of these structures in a totalizing praxis. Philosophy mediates in both. Praxis is in its movement a perfect totalization, but it always ends with only partial totalizations which in their turn will be transcended. The philosopher is the man who tries to understand these transcendences. . . . But I think that we are always *in transition*, always decompose while we produce and produce while we decompose: man is always "out of phase" with respect to those structures which condition him because he is also something else than that which makes him be what he is. That's why I don't understand why one wishes to stop with those structures. For me this is a logical scandal.[6]

5. La Quinzaine Littéraire, 16 mai, 1966, pp. 14–15.
6. "Jean-Paul Sartre Répond," *L'Arc*, no. 30, 1966, pp. 94 f.

7. *The Power of Discourse*

This scandal, however, does not follow of necessity from a structuralism which is aware of its own limitations. For in structuralism the distinction between language and speech or rather discourse is of great importance.

A. Martinet, a representative of structural linguistics, explains this distinction, which goes back to Ferdinand de Saussure, in the following way:

> It is absolutely necessary that the following be carefully distinguished: On the one hand, the linguistic facts of all kinds as they occur in expressions, on the other, the linguistic facts conceived as belonging to a supply which is at one's disposal for communication. It is not the task of the linguistic scientist to indicate the place where these linguistic facts are stored in the speaker or the event which induces the speaker to make a choice in keeping with his intentions of communication. But the linguistic scientist cannot escape assuming that there is a psycho-physiological arrangement which, while the child is learning the language—or later if it is a matter of an additionally learned language—becomes so conditioned that it enables him to analyze the experience to be communicated according to the norms of the language concerned and place the necessary possibilities of choice at his disposal at every moment of his expression. It is precisely this conditioning which is, in the proper sense, language. True, the availability of this language shows itself only in discourse or, if you wish, in acts of speaking. But discourse, acts of speaking, are not the language. The customary opposition of language and speech can be expressed in the concepts "code" and "report": the code is the arrangement which makes the composition of the report possible; and every part of a report is compared with this code in order to find its meaning.[7]

7. *Grundzüge der allgemeinen Sprachwissenschaft*, Stuttgart, 1963, pp. 32 f.

The question which imposes itself here in connection with our topic is whether discourse is merely a particular realization of the possibilities for combining the elements of a language; in which case I could pre-calculate all possible discourses and also all possible statements insofar as I succeed in ascertaining all elements of a language and all laws of combining them. Or is discourse not merely an ability to combine but also a creative activity by which the linguistic system can be endowed with new elements as well as new possibilities of combination?

Structuralism as a science operates, as a rule, only with the hypothesis that the system—in our case, the language—consists of a finite number of elements and a limited number of combinations. Only this working hypothesis allows it, by concentrating on the structurally fixed system, to conceive the system's structures in the purest possible way. From the start, the question of the creative activity of discourse is methodically abstracted from. But it is not answered in the negative and it must again be taken into account when the issue of the development of a language is raised.

As a matter of fact, it has already become evident from Sartre's argument with the structuralists that some structuralists are inclined to go beyond their working hypothesis, which favors the static system, and beyond the methodic abstraction from a possibly creative power of discourse. They tend to raise the superior power of language and the powerlessness of the speaker to a world-view.

8. *Prophecy and Proclamation as Combination*

Paying attention to the distinction between language and discourse, Christianity could make the following reflections.

(Some of these have already been suggested in the first section of this chapter about language.)

Is prophetic discourse only an ingenious gift for making combinations within the framework of a language in which mankind possesses already all elements of the revelation which is possible on the part of God? When we say that revelation is "closed" with Jesus Christ, can this mean that he has found and dared to express that combination which exhausts the relationship between "God" and "man" and beyond which nothing else can be combined: "God has become man"? Does Christian theology in this respect consist in the investigation and the development of this statement in its logical implications, presuppositions and consequences? And to what extent are these of a linguistic nature?

One can refer to the dogmatic system which has developed around the fundamental Christian formula, "God has become man," as "language" in opposition to the actual proclamation as "discourse." In that case is proclamation limited to merely repeating over and over again to different audiences the code of the dogmatic system as it has been drawn up? Or doesn't proclamation consist precisely in the ability of combination, and this in a plural way?

Sooner or later the proclaimer combines—or at least he tries to combine—from the dogmatic system, that answer which corresponds to the concrete questions of his listeners. Theology as a reflective science cannot directly give this answer because, like any science, it is not directly confronted with the situational question. Theology here has the task to check the answer which proclamation combines out of the system of faith, in order to see whether the combination is unobjectionable and how it can be integrated into the system as a valid new combination.

Another method of combination in proclamation is that of "alienation." When the proclamation is again and again also addressed to people who are already Christians and when they do not raise any special questions, experience shows that convictions and ways of acting can become empty through sheer routine. If the proclaimer before such an audience wishes to break through the walls of being-inured to the system and "knowing all that already," he will have recourse to the means of linguistic "alienation."[8] He will intentionally choose unusual and perhaps provocative combinations to arouse the interest of his listeners and to bring them closer again to the faith. The well-known use of "alienation" usually shows a poetic effect, which is described as follows by structural linguistics:

> These considerations allow us to characterize the vague impression that literary language is "more dense" than ordinary discourse somewhat more accurately. Like the deviations in question, the poetic secondary structures imprint on the language, on all levels of its structure, relations and configurations which regular grammar does not permit. This must also, but not in the first place, be understood in the sense of ornamental additions. The lengthened or shortened, broken or strangely connected structures of literary language fill the reservoir of untried models of thinking and seeing from which the general process of understanding does not cease to draw. They often become the source of change in the language itself.[9]

There is no doubt that this ability to combine, which the pro-

---

8. Cf. Hans-Dieter Bastian, *Verfremdung und Verkündigung*, Munich, 1965.
9. Manfred Bierwisch, "Strukturalismus. Geschichte, Probleme und Methoden," *Kursbuch* 5 (1966), p. 143.

claimer must have if he wishes to be effective, can be learned and practiced. One reason for the oft-mentioned disarray of today's Christian proclamation certainly lies in the fact that too little attention has been paid to this ability in the theological preparation of preachers and that, where attention was paid to it, it was usually done too amateurishly. The center of gravity in the curriculum still lies in the dogmatic, moral and legal system. This one-sidedness avenges itself in the fact that subsequently the preacher is without any method of putting the content of the system across.

Moreover, it also means that preachers whose native talent make them effective in this matter are not understood or misunderstood by the "followers of the system," and even treated with suspicion because of their correct and effective endeavors. The result of this is that the "followers of the system" are unable to make the creative and chamismatic statements of the proclamation fruitful for the systems, so that the latter stagnate and the dynamic movement given to them cannot make itself felt. Structuralistically speaking, language dominates to such an extent that its serving function with respect to discourse is forgotten; it thereby itself ceases to be a living language.

Chapter Four

SYSTEM AND DIFFERENCE

FROM WHAT WE HAVE SAID thus far about structuralism one can easily single out a key-word, viz., "system." This is not a coincidence. In structural analysis "system" is even a more central concept than is "structure." Paul Ricoeur, who has philosophically criticized structuralism, has drawn attention to this in connection with the linguistics of the School of Geneva:

> True, de Saussure did not use the term "structure" but the term "system." The term "structure," then, appeared as a specification of the system and indicated the restricting combinations which can be put into the foreground on the total field of possibilities of articulation and combination and which create the individual shape of a language. But in the adjectivistic form "structural" has become a synonym for system. In this way the structural viewpoint is globally opposed to the genetic viewpoint. It combined at the same time the idea of synchrony (the priority of the state of language over history), the idea of organism (language as a global unit which develops the parts), and finally the idea of the combination or "combinatorium" (language as a final order of different units). In this way the expression "the structure of a system" has led to the adjective "structural" to define the standpoint containing these different ideas, and finally to "structuralism" to indicate the investigations which take the struc-

turalistic viewpoint as their working hypothesis or even as an ideology and a weapon in controversy.[1]

1. *The Unconscious System*

Accordingly, what the structuralists want, even when in their investigations they go beyond language to other systems of signs, is the reconstruction of the system in which the individual phenomenon can at last be understood. As a rule, this system is not obvious, it is not something that at once discloses itself; on the contrary, it tends to conceal itself. Yet as long as the whole is not understood, the particular remains more or less unknown. For example, the things that internally prepared Lévi-Strauss for structuralism when he was still a student at the Sorbonne was his encounter with Marx, Freud and geology:

> All three showed that understanding consists in reducing one type of reality to another; they showed that the true reality is never the reality which most readily shows itself, and that the nature of the true indicates itself in the care it takes to conceal itself. In all these cases the same problem arises, viz., the relationship between what is sense perceptible and rational. The aim pursued also is the same, viz., a kind of super-rationalism intended to integrate the former into the latter without sacrificing anything of its properties.[2]

This quotation shows that as a rule one has to do with a plurality of systems, and that a system of relations is in its own way again an element in a broader system of relations, and so on.

---

1. "La structure, le mot, l'événement," *Esprit*, May 1967, p. 805.
2. *Tristes tropiques*, Paris, 1965, p. 44.

Lucien Goldmann, who devotes himself to sociology of literature and the critique of ideology in Paris, has applied this principle in a logical fashion to the explanation of the works of Pascal and Racine. He speaks as follows about the method:

> From these examples one can see how important the investigation of the meaningful structures of the history of ideological, social, political and economical movements can be and usually also is when one wishes to discern the coherence and inner structure of the literary, artistic or philosophical works connected with these movements. Fundamentally it is a matter of concretely applying two general principles which, in our opinion, should underlie every serious investigation in the historical and social sciences. These two principles are:
>
> 1. Every human phenomenon is embodied in a number of meaningful over-all structures, the discovery of which alone permits us to recognize its objective nature and significance.
>
> 2. In practice, in order to discern a constellation of individual data constituting such a meaningful structure and to distinguish the essential from the accidental in the immediate empirical data, one must incorporate these still little known data into a broader structure which encompasses the first structure; for instance, the writings of Pascal and Racine into the Jansenistic movement. But in this one should not forget that the provisional knowledge of the data from which one has started is one of the most important foundations by which we are able to discover the broader structure, precisely because those data constitute an element of this broader structure. For example, the writings of Pascal and Racine constitute the starting point of the hypothesis that there was an extreme Jansenism, and this discovery in its turn is an essential aid in the understanding of those works.[3]

---

3. *Recherches dialectiques*, Gallimard, Paris, 1959, pp. 114 f.

2. *Catholicity*

The standpoint of the "relative totality," of the system to which an element belongs and within which it must be understood, is of particular importance for Christianity. For catholicity, the aiming at the whole of the possible relationships, is a characteristic of the Christian world-view. All sectarianism, which isolates things and takes the part for the whole, is natively foreign to Christianity. But Christianity has not always been faithful in this matter. The structuralistic thesis that the individual is embedded in a certain system of relationships and must be understood in terms of this system is a challenge to Christianity to reflect anew on its own original catholicity.

When the modern physical sciences developed, a kind of positivism became rampant and identified what is immediately given with the truth even in the human sciences (*Geisteswissenschaften*). (This phase has, generally speaking, been overcome today in the physical sciences.) Theology and Christianity itself also largely fell for this tendency. One can see this trend in the way the Bible was read or in the reaction to modern exegesis when it tried with methods like those of structuralism to determine the place of details within the system and when it thus became evident that the detail had often to be understood in an entirely different way than had hitherto been customary. In dogmatic theology and in the catechisms built on this theology people had become much too much accustomed to use the Bible as a quarry from which they could cut the building blocks of their own system; they failed to pay attention to the formation from which these blocks came, and they neglected to ask whether, in view of their place within the system of the Bible, these blocks were able to perform the task assigned to them.

3. *"The Situation in Life"*

The very reconstruction of the "purely literary" totality demands that even in the case of the Bible one must go beyond the text and ask about its "situation in life" (*Sitz im Leben*), as the "form-historical" method expresses it. This is a category of the sociology of literature which I cannot renounce when I have become convinced that a work, even if it came from a single person, can be fully understood only against its social background. That's why one should not readily take over the radicalism which Roland Barthes has demanded for the science of literature, unless the requirement is strictly understood as a methodological directive wisely calling attention to the restriction of a standpoint, without of necessity implying a denial of the role played by the creative individual person. Barthes says:

> The history of literature is possible only if it is pursued sociologically, if it is interested in activities and institutions and not in individuals. . . . Writers are considered in it only as sharing in an institutional activity which transcends them as individuals, just as in so-called primitive societies the sorcerer participates in the magic function. This function, which is not laid down in any written law, can be understood only through the individuals who perform it; nevertheless, the function alone is the object of scientific investigation. The point, then, is to bring about in the history of literature as we know it a radical conversion, analogous to the one which has made possible the transition from royal chronicles to the writing of history in the proper sense. It is useless to supplement our literary chronicles

with a few new historical ingredients, with an unpublished source here and a more polished biography there. The framework itself must be exploded and the object turned around. Literature must be cut loose from the individual.[4]

Today one can say, of course, that progressive biblical scholarship has recognized and practised all this for a long time already, that it has overcome the one-sidedness of Barthes's tendency and has gone from "form-history" to "editorial history" in which again more attention is being paid to the individual author and editor. Nevertheless, it cannot be denied that even in exegesis reflection on the method and its consistent universal application are still far from attaining the necessary stringency. Most of all, however, the mentality in the other theological disciplines has not decisively changed—except in a few vanguard scholars— and the way in which the prevailing practice of preaching and scripture reading handles scriptural passages still brings to mind the well-known procedures of sectarian "bible scholars" rather than Christians who strive for catholicity.

4. *Dogmatic and Moral Theology*

With respect to dogmatics, the standpoint of totality cannot be done full justice by merely integrating a dogma into the totality of dogmas, by letting the light of all other dogmas shine on one dogma and thus preserving it from one-sided interpretation. For example, it is not enough to relate the statements about papal infallibity formulated by Vatican Council I to all other statements about this dogma known from the history of dogma and

---

4. *Sur Racine*, Paris, 1963, p. 165.

to the statements of Vatican Council II which indicate a dogmatic trend that must be taken seriously, even though it has not yet been formulated as a dogma. As has already been pointed out in the chapter on language, beyond all this I must place the dogma in its linguistic horizon and investigate this horizon. But this horizon reflects a very special social constellation having cultural, political, social and economic components. There have been very few attempts, at least within Christianity itself, to arrive at a deeper understanding of dogmatic evolution and of particular dogmas.

The standpoint of totality is particularly actual for morality, for the praxis of Christian life. Structuralistically speaking, it is impossible to judge any human deed in isolation from the system of reference in which it has been done. True, moral theology has always endeavored to elevate the context of an act to a methodological principle and to pay attention to the situation of an act. But in reality this often remained a purely theoretical postulate; it referred more to the abstract system of coherent moral principles and special precepts than to the concrete coherence system created by praxis. A structuralistic assessment would as a rule probably lead to the discovery of the over-all moral attitude of a human being in the individual moral acts (the subjective system) and to making the objective rightness of an act dependent on the real effect it has for the relative totality of the life to which it belongs (the objective system).

5. *Ideological Determinism*

Structuralism draws the attention of Christian morality to the fact that the individual moral act is in a way determined by the concrete system; it lets an idealistic conception of freedom be corrected by the insight that the system often leaves but little leeway. In spite of this, the Christian does not accept any absolute determinism or that kind of fatalism which flows from the allegedly total dependence on the system. The abolition of the subject, proclaimed by many structuralists, undoubtedly is a danger which threatens when the system becomes totalitarian. The assertion, however, that the systems must of necessity have or develop a totalitarian character cannot be proved structuralistically, but belongs to the ideology of the system; it is a thesis of a way of thinking that has succumbed to the system.

The position assumed by Christianity in this matter, which, in the final analysis, is a philosophical or theological standpoint, remains a challenge to a structuralism which, if Sartre's interpretation is correct, barely allows any initiative to the subject:

The disappearance or, in Lacan's own words, the "de-centering" of the subject is connected with the discrediting of history. If there is no longer any praxis, there can no longer be a subject. What do Lacan and the psychoanalysts who follow him tell us? Man does not think, he is thought, even as for certain linguists he is spoken. In this view the subject no longer occupies the center. He is an element among other elements, and the essential point is the "layer" or, if you prefer, the structure in which he is caught and which constitutes him.

This idea comes from Freud, who already assigned an ambiguous place to the subject. Sandwiched between the "id" and the "super-ego," the human subject, as seen by the psychoanalyst, a little resembles de Gaulle between the Soviet Union and the U.S.A. The ego does not exist in itself, it is constructed, and its role remains purely passive. It is not an actor but a meeting-place, the locus of conflicting forces. The analyst does not demand his patient to act; on the contrary, he asks him to let himself be activated by surrendering to his free associations.[5]

6. *Differential Relationships*

If we ask how structuralism could arrive at this ideological exaggeration in which the subject is negated, then the key-word is the term "difference." For in the system of signs to be analyzed the structuralist no longer holds the naive view that the sign represents a thing; no, the sign, on the one hand, is defined by its oppositional relationship to all other signs, and on the other, it is understood in itself as a purely inner, immanent difference.[6] We may illustrate this point with a typical reference taken from de Saussure. It is concerned with language, but for structuralists language is the primordial model of all structural systems.

In language, de Saussure tells us, there are only differences. What is more, a difference generally implies positive terms between which the difference is set up, but in language there are only differences without positive terms. Whether one considers the signified or the signifier, language has neither ideas nor sounds existing before the linguistic system, but only conceptual and phonic differences that have arisen from the system. The idea or phonic matter contained in a sign is less important than the other signs around it. Proof of this is that the value of a term may be changed without either its meaning or its sound being affected, solely because a neighboring term has been changed.[7]

---

5.   "Jean-Paul Sartre Répond," *L'Arc*, no. 30, 1966, pp. 91 f.

6.   Cf. Paul Ricoeur, "La structure, le mot, l'évémenent," *Esprit*, May, 1967, pp. 804 f.

7.   *Course in General Linguistics*, p. 120.

Lévi-Strauss, who made this thesis the foundation of his method to explain totemism, came to this result:

> [Totemism also] consists in the union of two opposite concepts. With the aid of a special vocabulary formed from the names of plants and animals—this is its only distinct feature—so-called totemism expresses in its own way, or as we would say today, with the aid of a special code, mutual relations and oppositions, which could also be given a different form. For example, among some tribes of North and South America it is done through the opposition of heaven and earth, war and peace, above and below, red and white, etc. The most general model of these opposites and their most systematic usage can perhaps be found in China in the two principles "Yang" and "Yin"; they stand for male and female, day and night, summer and winter, from the union of which emerges an organized whole (*tao*), viz., the married couple, a whole day or a full year. Thus totemism can be reduced to a special way of formulating a general problem: one must proceed in such a way that the opposition, rather than being an obstacle, serves to bring about integration.[8]

7. Dualism in Christianity?

The ideology of structuralism considers, without examination, the laws of the structural to be reflexes of the structurell; it rashly transfers conclusions drawn from the level of signs to that of the reality intended by these signs. When one does not fall into this ideology, then the structuralistic thesis that the elements of a system are constituted by their difference[9] can also

---

8. *Das Ende des Totemismus*, Frankfurt a.m., 1965, pp. 115 f.

9. In language, as in any semiological system, says de Saussure, whatever distinguishes one sign from the others, also constitutes it. Difference creates character, just as it creates value and the unit. *Op. cit.*, p. 121.

be of service to the self-understanding of Christianity as a system of religious meaning.

A certain conceptual dualism is found in all religious systems, Christianity included; e.g., the opposition of heaven and earth, body and soul, nature and the supernatural. This dualism could be investigated to see how it, too, is to be accounted for by the general rule of human sign-systems that a sign exists by the fact of being different from other signs (as is obvious in the case of opposites).

On the other hand, Christianity objects to the absolute dualism according to which a divine principle of good and a contrary principle of evil are the constituent elements of the world. This implies that man is not absolutely subject to the systematics of sign-systems working with difference and opposition. At the same time, one can see how even highly developed civilizations in their religious, political and philosophical systems over and over again lapse into a fateful dualism; the latter is simply transferred from the structural to the structurell, without corresponding to "objective reality."

8. *The Subject as I-You Relationship*

With respect to man as a subject also, the Christian can learn from structuralism and its theory of difference. What makes man man is his power to develop an I-consciousness. But this power is not actuated outside a language, and the elements of this language are defined by their difference from the others. What constitutes man on the level of consciousness as an I is, as a matter of fact, the discovery of the You, and this discovery belongs first and foremost to the realm of language because language introduces us to the world and opens it up to us. And all further development of the I-consciousness is an unfolding of the differences in which I stand with respect to the rest of the world. This, too, primarily comes about as conditioned by language with its dualistic "world-view."

The Christian also may be very much convinced that, insofar as the "objective reality" of the human subject is concerned, the individual exists through his relationship to the whole and as individual is destined by the difference for other human beings. Nevertheless, he will be on his guard against the structuralistic ideology that man is nothing but a bundle of relationships at the mercy of the system and nothing but the negation of the others. Such a position would fail to do justice to the creative power of man which enables him personally to assume a standpoint toward his relationships and personally also to influence his differences.

Chapter Five

THE SIGNIFIER AND THE SIGNIFIED

BEING CONCERNED with the systems of signs, structuralism has devoted special attention to the structure of the sign. The fundamental distinction which it discovered in the sign is that between the signifier and the signified. The signifier (*signifiant*) is that part of the sign which "materializes," which is "perceptible," visible or audible; and the signified (*signifié*) is the part of the sign which is "hidden," "immaterial," its "meaning." To connect this with the last concept discussed in the preceding chapter, the sign is the difference between signifier and signified; hence to the extent that this difference disappears, the sign ceases to be a sign. It becomes a pure concept, sheer "thought" when the signified triumphs, just as it becomes merely "something there," a mere "thing" when the signifier predominates. The sign is a sign by virtue of being a "thing of thought"—an expression that should, of course, be properly understood here.

Explaining the above-mentioned distinction, Roland Barthes writes:

> Accordingly, I want to repeat that every semiology postulates a relationship between two terms, one of which is the "signifier" and the other the "signified." This relationship is concerned with objects of

different orders and therefore not a relationship of equality but of equivalence. In accepted parlance, the "signifier" simply *expresses* the "signified." In contrast to this, however, it should be kept in mind that in any semiological system one does not deal with two but with three different terms. For I do not at all grasp one term after the other but the correlation which connects them. Accordingly, there are the *signifier*, the *signified* and the *sign*, which is the associative totality of the first two terms. For example, take a bunch of roses and let them signify my passion. But aren't there here only a signifier and a signified, the roses and my passion? Not even that; there are only my "passionalized" roses. But on the analytical level there are three concepts, for the roses "full' of passion certainly can be analyzed into roses and passion. Both existed before they united and formed the third object, the sign. Just as in real life I cannot separate the roses from their message, so on the analytical level I cannot equate the roses as signifier with the roses as sign: the signifier is empty, the sign is full, it has meaning. To give another example, let us take a black stone. I can let this stone signify in several ways, but when finally I assign a particular meaning to it—for instance, a death sentence in an anonymous casting of votes—it becomes a sign.[1]

1. *Sacraments as Signs*

Christianity may not neglect to reflect on the structure of signs because its sacraments clearly are signs. If one takes seriously the view that it is proper to a sign to consist of a "matter" which is neutral with respect to meaning (the signifier) but to which a certain meaning (the signified) has been attached, then the following conclusion must be drawn: from the mere "matter" of a sign I cannot with certainty infer its meaning, but I must ask what meaning has been attached to the "matter" in the case

---

1. *Mythologies*, ed. du Seuil, Paris, 1957, pp. 219 f.

of this sign; in other words, I must ask the one who created this sign.

For example, it is methodically wrong if one tries to "read" the signs of bread and wine in the celebration of the Eucharist by referring to the "essence" or function of bread and wine, as if bread and wine directly express what is meant. Bread and wine would then not be the signifier, the material element of a sign whose meaning must be ascertained from elsewhere; they would give expression to nothing but themselves, so that we would no longer be on the level of the sign.

Similarly, the meaning which bread and wine have in the celebration of the Eucharist cannot be simply derived from parallels in the history of religion, for I would then tacitly presuppose that the "matter" of bread and wine always imposes the same meaning on the founder of the sign. Parallels from the history of religion are useful if I can show that Jesus of Nazareth has intended exactly the same meaning which in other religions also are attached to bread and wine in a cultic context.

What bread and wine in the Eucharist are signs of is a matter which we must ascertain from the one who has given this signifier its signified. At any rate, one cannot appeal to the allegedly "natural" meaning of bread and wine or to the meaning which they have in other, non-Christian religions in order to oppose the meaning which they happen to have received from their founder in Christianity. One who creates a sign has the freedom to provide the signifier with a signified of his own choice. At most, one could wonder whether another signifier would not have been more appropriate as the bearer of a particular signified. But this is another problem, which we will not consider here.

2. The "Substance" of the Sign "the Eucharist"

The distinction between the three terms, the sign, its signifier and its signified, can draw attention to a danger inherent in dealing with a system of signs, viz., the possibility that one will unwittingly take signs out of this system and interpret them on a different level. The consequence of this would be that one unwittingly but nonetheless truly misinterprets the sign. This danger exists especially when one deals with a symbolic action, a dynamic event which takes place on the sign level, or constitutes a particular sign system.

The celebration of the Christian Eucharist again can serve as an example of this danger. This celebration is a cultic act, in which under signs there occurs an encounter between God and man. The entire celebration is a single sign unfolding around the signs of bread and wine. Thus we are dealing here with a sign system. From the first moment that bread and wine enter the picture, they must be understood as signs. They no longer express themselves, but as signifiers are open for any meaning. Their "substance," to use a traditional expression, which they used to have as bread and wine plays no role; the point of interest lies in their "substance" as signs. Now, the "substance" of the sign is identical with the signified of the sign, with its meaning.

Pursuing this approach, in which bread and wine are seen as signs within the celebration of the Christian Eucharist, we note that there is a change in meaning; the signified becomes different. In the so-called "preparation of the gifts" bread and wine mean the participants in the celebration themselves; they place themselves at God's disposal in this form, they express their willingness to recognize God's rule over their lives. God's response to this willingness of man to surrender himself is God's own surrender to man which finds expression in the so-called "change," in the fact that a new signified is spoken over the signs of bread and wine: "This is my body and my blood," in the sense that bread and wine now mean man's life insofar as this life has been accepted by God and become the life of God himself. The intermediary, mediator and primordial type of this union of God with man is Christ; that's why sharing in God's life means the same as sharing in Christ's life. Thus the full meaning of bread and wine is the life of Christ in which our life has been taken up in order to share in God's life. The sign of bread and wine, endowed with this meaning, is returned to the participants in the celebration in the so-called "communion"; the latter itself is once more a sign that God's life becomes united with the life of man.

Misunderstandings are bound to occur whenever for any reason whatsoever it is forgotten that the figures of bread and wine occurring in the celebration of the Eucharist do not "express" bread and wine and that bread and wine are only signifiers which during the symbolic act are given several signifieds, "loaded" with meanings. With respect to the "change," this forgetfulness has as its result that the "transsubstantiation" is made to refer to the substance which bread and wine have when they are not signs but merely bread and wine. Such a view means that the cultic act, which is a single sign system, is left behind and that one passes from the level of signs to another level; consequently, one interrupts the symbolic act and even disrupts it. The mistake consists in the disregarding of one of the main rules of semiology, the science of the sign: individual elements can be correctly interpreted only within the system to which they belong, and one may not arbitrarily change from one level to another.[2]

3. *Ambiguity and Openness*

The question must also be raised whether there aren't signs and sign systems in which the signifiers are provided with an ambiguous signified, so that it is left to the reader to give it a uniform meaning. One can even ask whether there aren't signs which offer only a signifier and expect the reader to provide this signifier with a signified, and thereby to constitute the sign as sign.

Roland Barthes discusses this point in connection with great literature and the task of literary criticism; and according to him, criticism should set itself the following goal:

It should not endeavor to decipher the meaning of the work studied but rather reconstruct the rules and the restriction under which this literary meaning has been developed. At the same time, however, it should realize that the literary work of art is a very self-willed semantic system, the purpose of which is to bring into the world *meaning in general* and not only *a particular meaning*. The literary work of

---

2. There is question here only of *one* aspect of the Eucharistic celebration and it is offered here by way of an example and model of a structural analysis, viz., what is the "substance" of a sign, and in what sense can one speak of a "transsubstantiation" in a dynamic sign system? The question of the sense in which that condition to which the sign refers is a matter of "real presence" lies beyond the competence of structural analysis (cf. the chapter, the Structurell and the Structural). It belongs to philosophy and theology to clarify what kind of realization of a condition can be connected with a sign and what kind of presence Christ, the founder of the Eucharistic sign, has, as a matter of fact, connected with this sign.

art, at least, the kind which the critic usually considers (perhaps a definition of "good" literature is implied in this), is never totally meaningless, but mysterious or "inspired"; neither is it ever perfectly clear. It has, if you wish, an uncertain-dependent meaning. As a matter of fact, it offers itself to the reader as a really *signifying* system, but withdraws from him as *signified* object.

This kind of *dé-ception* or *dé-prise* of the meaning explains, on the one hand, why the literary work of art is so powerful in asking the world questions; it shatters the established values, which are so strongly protected by the world-views, the ideologies and sound reason. But the work of literary art itself can never answer these questions, for a great work is hardly ever "dogmatic." On the other hand, we have here also the reason why the work of art lends itself again and again to new interpretations; for ultimately there is no reason why people would ever stop to discuss Racine or Shakespeare, except perhaps at some time because of a sudden emotional reaction, which in its turn then again would be a kind of language.

Because literature constantly offers meanings and these meanings are at the same time always "elusive," literature is nothing but a kind of *language*, i.e., a system composed of signs; its meaning does not lie in the communication but rather in this *system*. This is the reason why the literary critic's task is not to reproduce the communication of the work but only the system in question, just as it is not the task of the linguist to decipher the meaning of a sentence but to determine the formal structure which alone makes the transmission of that meaning possible.

As a matter of fact, it is only when literary criticism comes to the realization that it itself embodies only a kind of "language" or, more accurately expressed, a "metalanguage," that literary criticism is able to be, in a contradictory but nonetheless authentic way, both objective and subjective, historical and existentiell, totalitarian and liberal. For, on the one hand, the language which each critic has chosen for himself has not come over him as a kind of heavenly sent inspiration but rather as one of those languages which are offered to him by his epoch; it is objectively the expression of a particular historical maturity of knowledge, ideas and intellectual passions; in other words, it is a *necessity*. On the other hand, this necessary language is also chosen by each critic for a particular existentiell model; for example, as a means for exercising one of his own spiritual functions, in which he then lays down his whole "depth," i.e., his preference, his pleasure, his resistance, his obsession. In this way the dialogue between two historical situations and between two subjective spheres—that of the author and that of the critic—can begin in the midst of the critical work itself. Nevertheless, this dialogue refers to the presence in a wholly egoistic fashion: literary criticism is neither a "homage" to the truth of the past nor one to the truth of "the other," but is the building-up of that which in our time can be understood.[3]

4. *Bad Clarity of Meaning in the Explanation of the Bible*

In its own eyes, Christianity has to announce a truth, and that's why it tries to speak with the greatest possible unity of meaning, to be as unambiguous as possible. The danger in this is that it may become fanatic in its attempts to be unambiguous and adhere to a dogmatism which is solely interested in holding fast to truths. But why should it be prohibited that a truth could consist in drawing attention to the ambiguity and openness of a reality?

This problem reveals itself very clearly in dealing with the Bible. It is difficult for Christianity to admit that the Bible in many respects lacks the desired unambiguity. One could wonder whether there is perhaps a theological ground for this ambiguity, whether perhaps this very ambiguity itself is already a divine revelation and whether the desire for unambiguity is in every respect theologically justifiable. Instead of reflecting on these

---

3. *Op. cit.* (footnote 4 of Ch. 2), pp. 25 f.

questions, theologians keep falling into the temptation to give an unambiguous meaning to the texts and fix them dogmatically. But the resulting clarity of meaning can only be a "bad" clarity; it attempts to give an *answer* where the text perhaps wished to raise only a *question*; or it points to *one* road where the text itself indicates that *several* roads are possible. To impose an unambiguous interpretation on an ambiguous, "open" scriptural text would, in the eyes of the Christian, mean to change God's openness into man's narrow-mindedness, God's truth into man's untruth, God into an idol.

Precisely when one realizes that many biblical texts are close to the literary work of art, one should from the very start look for their "general meaning," instead of getting lost in the hopeless attempt to discover a "particular meaning" as their objective truth. And when, nonetheless, one finds a "particular meaning," then one should investigate whether this meaning is not a message which has arisen from the fact that I have approached the text with my language and its questions and then made the text answer in kind. The "particular meaning" which arises in this way is, as an objective-subjective "truth," not a truth of a lesser rank; having arisen from the dialogue of the Bible with the reader, it is that truth which is ultimately intended because this truth alone is a living and life-giving truth. And this is precisely what the Bible wants.

5. *"Facts" and Interpretation in the Gospels*

The distinctions made in this chapter also throw a clarifying light on the question why the statements of the gospels are proclamation texts. They are concerned with proclamation if the Bible understands and proposes the life of Jesus as a sign. If the events of his life had been "objectively" recorded, they would merely have been a signifier, a possible bearer of meaning, the "matter" which could have been interpreted in this or that way. It is only when someone himself assigns a meaning to his action or when others do this that the event becomes a sign, a signifier provided with a signified. To demand that a biblical text which explicitly wishes to pass on the meaning of Jesus's life abstain from giving this meaning and limit itself to "facts" is fundamentally to misunderstand the Bible. And to read the reports about the life of Jesus as if everything were merely a matter of "facts" is making the same mistake. The Bible reports are reports about the life of Jesus as a sign, with respect to which the events are the signifiers which the report has already provided with a signified. The more the signifier and the signified merge and become one, the more successful the sign is. The fact that it is so difficult to separate event and meaning in the Bible argues not against the Bible but for it, on condition that one measures every literary work by the genus to which it belongs.

On the other hand, against many structuralistical exaggerations, Bible-oriented Christianity will hold fast to the position that one cannot arbitrarily assign signifieds to the signifiers; it will even claim that the subjective endeavor to give things a meaning is the attempt to conceal the "objective meaning" of the state of affairs. The meaning, the interpretation of the life of Jesus, as well as the meaning, the interpretation of the reports about him must be adapted to the structure of life and that of the report, the signified and the signifier must be brought into a kind of harmony if the sign is to be convincing. The sign can become incredible both through over-interpretation which cannot abstain from a certain dogmatic exegesis, and through under-interpretation, as found in many contemporary attempts of demythologization.

The question of the function of the theological sciences as compared to the task of the practical proclamation of the faith has already been touched upon in a previous chapter. If we apply the distinction between the signifier and the signified to this question, one could say: proclamation is the attempt to make the signifier Jesus Christ, as represented to us by the Bible and Christian tradition, a living and convincing sign for the situation that actually exists at any given time by providing this signifier with a signified in keeping with the time; in other words, proclamation must describe Jesus Christ for the contemporary mentality in the language of the audience.

Theology, on the other hand, must see to it that Jesus Christ as a signifier is always "at our disposal," that he does not become forgotten and is not passed on in a distorted way. Moreover, it must check whether the contemporary signified, assigned to him by proclamation, does justice to him; in other words, theology verifies the validity of the sign of Christ which the proclamation of any era newly creates, in order to see wheher the signified appropriate to the era has preserved the structures of the original Christian signified. For the latter is, in the eyes of the Christian, the permanent norm governing all subsequent descriptions.

Chapter Six

"WAY OF WRITING" AND SILENCE

IT IS AGAIN ROLAND BARTHES to whom we owe a penetrating description of what is to be understood by the "way of writing." In between language and style there is in any literary form a so-called "way of writing," which he describes as follows:

> [It is] the general choice of a tone or, if you prefer, an ethos; and it is precisely in this that an author unambiguously shows his individuality, for he himself is involved. Language and style precede all problematics of the personal way of expression (*langage*). Language and style are natural products of the time and the biological person. The formal identity of the author, however, truly unfolds only outside the established grammatical norms and constants of style. It unfolds there where what is written, which at first is gathered together in a linguistically wholly innocent form, first becomes a total sign, the choice of a human way of acting, the affirmation of a certain good, thus committing the writer to make a certain happiness or misfortune evident and to communicate it and, at the same time, connecting the form—both normal and exclusive—of what he says (*parole*) with the wider history of the others. Language and style are blind forces, but the "way of writing" is an act of historical solidarity; language and style are objects, but the "way of writing" is a function. It is the relation between what the writer creates and society; it is the literary way of expression (*langage*), transformed by its social destination;

it is the form grasped in its human intention, which thereby is connected with the great crises of history.[1]

1. *Faith, the Christian "Way of Writing" and Morality*

Transferred to world-view systems in the more restricted sense, particularly to Christianity, the "way of writing" corresponds to that individual attitude which in Christian terms is called "faith." Faith is one's personal involvement within the Christian system. The assertion that this faith has a personal style is self-evident. This style is conditioned by the intellectual and characteristic qualities of the individual; it is not directly a moral category. It is also self-evident that this Christian faith must come about within the Christian world-view and its language if it wishes to be explicit faith. Faith, the individual form of commitment to Christ, if it wishes to be meaningful, must "come about" in language and style, in the general and individual growing into Christianity; there must be the will to make the language and style of being-a-Christian my own by a personal act, so that these are no longer merely "at hand"; they must be made an object of my freedom.

This happens when I consciously begin to use the language I've learned, when I choose the Christian view among the possible world-views as the medium for my way of looking at the world. The development of this way begins when I express my*self* through the language of Christianity, formulate *my* questions and search for *my* answers. While I combine the possibilities allowed by the language of the system for the expression of

---

1. *Le degré zéro de l'écriture*, ed. du Seuil, Paris, 1953, pp. 23 f.

the I which as this individual I irrevocably am, there arises a unique personal way of believing, and this way expresses itself in a particular way of writing and speaking.

The more lively one's faith is, the more individual also this faith and the world of faith is. This leads to the paradoxical phenomenon that when a system becomes a living possession of many, its unity is seemingly put into jeopardy. In reality, however, the resulting pluralism of individual forms of faith confirms that the system offers room in which the individual way of looking at the world can find expression. It would be worthwhile to investigate to what extent many Christian "heresies" and "sects" were at first nothing but legitimate ways of expressing and living the faith by markedly strong individuals, whom the system subsequently, through a mistaken ideology of unity, forced to settle elsewhere and who only then lost their bond with the whole and assumed the character of a sect.

The structural category of "the way of writing" also makes it possible to show faith as man's fundamental decision and thus connect morality with faith. The act of faith by which I decide for a certain world-view, committing and entrusting myself to it, is the fundamental moral decision *par excellence*. By this decision I enter history as one who acts with responsibility, at least if human history consists in this that man endeavors to be in harmony with the whole, takes a position in its respect and decides on a project of the future. Wherever markedly personal ways of being-a-believer occur, one must from the outset count on it that we are living in an era where history is on the move; the system will inevitably be shaken by these new ways but, at the same time, it will also be given a new lease on life and influence on history. Such an era will be a time of "moral rearmament," of "moral renewal" of the system and of history.

2. *Faith, the Formation of Groups Against Entropy*

It is only by faith that I enter the community of faith, the groups of believers who are characterized by distinct ways of being-a-believer. It is only by this act of individualization within the system of faith that my socialization with the other believers succeeds and I achieve solidarity with the system. The most loyal servants of the system are not the people who, out of respect for the system, do not dare to bring their personality to bear on it, but those who do precisely that, even if on occasion it may seem that they thereby put the system itself into question. The poet whose use of language seems to do violence to it is precisely the man who exhaustively exploits its ultimate possibilities and, at the same time, gives this language its most beautiful affirmation. The system of Christian faith also does not live by its theologians and functionaries, who must keep the system as system in mind, but by its believers (among whom we must, of course, also include the theologians and officials). But only faith, the moral commitment, which is impossible without being an individual and individualized confession, constitutes a "people of God"; this people the system must serve, and from this people the system derives the justification for its existence.

The choice of a "way of writing," says Roland Barthes, "means the choice of a social realm in which the writer wishes to situate the nature of his *langage*. . . . His choice is a decision of conscience and not one of efficacy."[2] This holds also for faith. To the extent that I take it seriously, I choose my companions

---

2. *Op. cit.*, p. 26.

in the faith and isolate myself from others within the same system of faith. Every personal decision of faith is an affirmation of those who are like-minded and a challenge to the other-minded; it leads to the formation of corresponding groups. In this respect Christianity's system of faith is of necessity a structure with built-in tensions; its unity results from the plurality of more or less informal groups of believers. Any attempt to do away with these tensions is a levelling process and leads to the "heat death" of the community of faith. In this respect Lévi-Strauss is right when he describes man's creation of systems as a fateful undertaking:

> [The creator of a system] works at the dissolution of an original order and thus puts organized matter into a condition of increasing inertia which one day will be final. Since man began to breathe and provide for himself, from the discovery of fire to the invention of atomic and thermonuclear machines, man has done nothing—aside from his self-reproduction—but destroy billions of structures which can never again be restored. True, he has built cities and cultivated fields, but here, too, one finds only "machines" destined to produce inertia at a rate entirely out of proportion to the mass of organization implied by these cities and fields. . . . In this way the whole of civilization can be described as one enormously complex mechanism; we would like to see in it the possibilities, the chance for survival possessed by our world, but in reality its sole task is to produce what physicists call entropy, that is to say, inertia. Every word exchanged, every line printed establishes a connection between two partners and levels a relationship which hitherto had been characterized by differences of views and therefore by greater organization. Instead of being called "anthropology" it ought to be named "entropology," a term which designates the discipline for the investigation of the process of disintegration in the highest forms of its appearance.[3]

---

3. *Tristes tropiques*, pp. 447 f.

3. *About the "Distress" of Faith: Tradition, Revolution,
    Tolerance*

On the other hand, a structural outlook which takes its starting point in the linguistic model is from the very outset a safe-
guard against overestimating the freedom of one's moral commitment within a particular system. Roland Barthes writes:

> It is impossible for the writer to select his "way of writing" in a
> kind of warehouse of timeless literary forms. The possible "ways of
> writing" of a particular author originate under the pressure of history
> and tradition. There is a history of "ways of writing" but this history
> is of a twofold nature. At the very moment when general history pro-
> poses—or imposes—a new problematics of the literary way of ex-
> pression, the "way of writing" remains still full of reminiscences of
> past usage. For language is never virginal; words possess a second
> memory and reminiscences which in a mysterious way maintain them-
> selves in the midst of new meanings. The "way of writing" is pre-
> cisely the compromise between freedom and remembrances, it is the
> remembering freedom which is freedom only in the gesture of choice
> but no longer in its duration.[4]

The Christian finds it distressing that he must spell out his
personal faith in a language saturated with tradition. It is as if I
must do a running battle with the language when I wish to un-
fold my vision of the faith in it. It cannot be done without misunderstandings on both sides. My choice of terms reveals itself
as unfortunate because I haven't done justice to their meaning
in the system; and on the other hand, the system misunderstands
my new combination or formation of words in the sense of the

---

4. *Op. cit.* (in footnote 4 of Ch. 2), pp. 19 f.

traditional patterns or else as intolerable deviations. And if I succeed in sufficiently expressing what I mean, then the formulation of my ideas acts as a sponge, it soaks up all kinds of meanings which I did not at all intend. The wish to keep it as young and pure as on its first day is hopeless. It cannot be preserved, except as "preserves" are kept. It becomes part of the system as a successful or unsuccessful structure and establishes a tradition. By the very fact it ceases to express *my* faith, so that I have to start all over again. One always has to start all over again. Precisely because the system is constantly trying to seize me, it constantly challenges me in my freedom to save my vision of the faith from the system and thus to keep myself and my vision alive.

The "ways of writing" can be structuralistically classified by their relationship to language. There is a more traditional "way of writing" and a more revolutionary way because there are people with more traditional dispositions and others who are more revolutionary. Their commitment corresponds to these dispositions, and the system needs both. Something similar applies to faith in Christianity. The faith of all Christians should be a faith that is personally acquired and personally developed, but the way in which it stands in opposition to the traditional structures of the system is different. Some people add a new brightness to the old structures, while others question them. That's why it is wrong to declare that one's own vision of faith is binding on all, wrong to try to make one's own faith a system. Such an attitude would condemn this faith to death and do an injustice to the others. Moreover, it would also try to compete with the system common to all. In this matter the faithful must practice that mutual tolerance which they expect the official system to practice with respect to their own vision of the faith.

4. *Silence as a Confession of the Faith*

The distress of the "way of writing" can give rise to the temptation not to write any longer, not because of a lack of commitment and morality, but for the sake of the authenticity of one's commitment. The distress experienced in the attempt to "correctly" articulate one's faith can lead to its renunciation—not the renunciation of the faith itself but its "profession." A writer's silence can be very eloquent; similarly, a believer who does not articulate his faith can by this very act profess it. Many types of atheism are nothing but awkward or aggressive forms of a believing silence. Doesn't precisely modern man with his scepticism toward catch-words in literature and religion prefer silence to the word that is untrue or liable to be misunderstood? The sobriety with words which characterizes the physical scientist when he has to speak of matters pertaining to the world-view is not merely the result of a lack of training but also a professional distrust of empty discourse. There exists a danger that the language of the official professions of faith also will become an object of the justified protest against the language used in preaching, prayerbooks, hymns and worship, which is experienced as untrue and inauthentic. These creeds should be tested to see to what extent their language can be adapted to the modern believer without doing violence to their substance; otherwise modern man's personal profession of faith will be condemned to silence or will needlessly have to deviate too much from the official language.

This can perhaps be done by reformulating the substance of the Christian system of faith in a language containing as little "history" as possible, a language which tries to achieve a "neutral way of writing."[5] This is what Roland Barthes recommends to the modern writer:

> [All these traditional "ways of writing"] imply a "density" of the form and presuppose a problematics of the linguistic expression and of society because they posit the word as an object, something to be worked on by a manual laborer, a sorcerer or a clerk, but not by an intellectual. But the neutral "way of writing" actually reproduces the first condition of classical art, viz., its instrumental character. But now this formal instrument is no longer in the service of a triumphant ideology; it is the way there exists a new situation for the writer, it is the way there can be silence, it freely renounces any recourse to elegance and adornment, for both of these dimensions would reintroduce the element of time into the "way of writing," and time is a diverting power, the bearer of history. If the "way of writing" is really neutral, if the form of expression, instead of being a troublesome and indomitable act, assumes the character of a pure equation which, in view of man's emptiness, has no other "density" than an algebraic problem, then literature is overcome, the human problematics is discovered and represented without any coloring. The writer is again a sincere man.[6]

One should ignore the ideological undertone of Barthes manifesting itself in the words "man's emptiness." And one should also realize that there are limits which prevent the object of faith from being equated with a mathematically univocal formula.

---

5. We abstract here from the fact that our need for such a "way of writing" itself again is something "historical."

6. *Op. cit.* (in footnote 4, Ch. 2), p. 72 f.

If this is done, however, the "neutral way of writing" is a valid demand addressed to the contemporary proclamation of the faith if this proclamation wishes to be of assistance to the modern believer in the articulation of his personal profession of the faith.

Chapter Seven

MYTH AND IDEOLOGY

THE "NEUTRAL WAY of writing" could also be called a
" 'way of writing' interested in demythologization," at least if
the term "myth" is structuralistically understood[1] as a particular
form in which something is said and not as the *content* of what
is said. Any statement whatsoever can become a myth; this happens when the statement no longer intends an object, as it does
in the primary sign system; it is no longer an object language,
but the statement—even one which, considered in itself, intends
an object—is taken up into a secondary semiological system and
there becomes the bearer of a meaning which is no longer un-
conditionally tied to the object-meaning which it has in the object language. (As a rule, however, it retains a connection with
that meaning.) Roland Barthes gives the following example:

I am waiting my turn at the hairdresser and someone gives me a
copy of *Paris-Match.* On the cover a young Negro in French uniform

---

1. A first condition for not misunderstanding a text is, according to the structuralistic standpoint, that one must endeavor to understand a concept in the sense
in which it has been determined in the system to which it belongs. We must
explicitly remind the reader that the concept "myth" as used in the following
pages must not be understood in the sense of Bultmann or any kind of philosophy of religion.

gives the military salute, with his eyes looking up toward a crease in the *tricouleur*. This is the *meaning* of the picture. Naive or not, I clearly realize what it should tell me: France is a great empire; all its sons, regardless of color, faithfully serve under its flag; and there exists no better argument against the opponents of an alleged colonialism than the zeal of this young Negro to serve his alleged oppressors. Here also, then, there is a wider semiological system: it contains a signifier, which itself has been created by a preceding system, *viz., a colored soldier makes the French military salute*; it contains a signified, viz., that there is here an intentional mixture of being-French and being-a-soldier; and finally it contains the *presence* of the signified throughout the signifier.[2]

Accordingly, a myth in the structuralistic sense is a statement in which the sign of a primary semiological system becomes the signifier of a secondary system; the latter provides it with a new signified, and together with this it constitutes a new sign, the myth.

Roland Barthes describes three attitudes toward the myth. The first of these is that of the one who creates the myth. What he has in mind is the signified of the myth—in the above-mentioned example, the French empire—and looks for a suitable signifier which can serve as an example, a symbol—the saluting Negro. This attitude is analytic; it is unable to let the myth exercise its influence because it is one's own creation and one sees through its intention. This attitude easily ends in cynicism.

The second attitude, which is also analytic, is that of the mythologist. He deciphers the myth, discloses the deformity and the "abuse" committed with the sign of the object-language; he unmasks the intention of the myth—in this case, the saluting

---

2. *Mythologies*, p. 223.

Negro as the alibi for the French empire. He, too, can no longer naively accept the myth; he fundamentally has a demythologizing attitude.

The third attitude is that of the reader without a reflective mentality. The myth succeeds with him because it can let its mechanisms play their role without being disturbed. The attitude is dynamic; the reader lets himself be influenced and carried away. He lives the myth as it was intended, that is to say: the saluting Negro is neither an example or symbol nor an alibi; he is the realization of French empirehood.[3]

1. *Metalanguage as Christian Self-criticism*

Christianity gives a certain meaning to the world and endeavors to express this meaning by signs borrowed from object-language. Thus it shares in the mythological creations existing in this language. But precisely Christianity must constantly check to see that it does not do violence to the things of the object-language. Christianity cannot afford to deal in a prejudicious way with the object-language and ascribe to the signs of language meanings which are far-fetched or even entirely foreign to them. For Christianity wants precisely to point out that the world of things, as described by the object-language, is "objectively" open to deeper meanings; it wants to show the depth dimension of that world. If this is to succeed, one must carefully examine the signs in their other dimension and avoid everything which can make them turn in on themselves because they feel misused.

---

3. Cf. *Mythologies*, pp. 224 f.

How often hasn't it happened that rash and self-secure Christians gave things a meaning which, on closer inspection, they did not have! For example, some Christians have deified nature and called technical progress diabolical; others attributed man's deed to God and, when man failed, they promptly saw in this the work of the devil.

Precisely because theology and religious discourse in general are a metalanguage, precisely because they cast over the object-language a second network of meanings which cannot easily be verified in man's dealing with things, intensive self-control is necessary, as well as a strong discipline of speech, which only a keen internal and external critique can seem to guarantee. Christianity needs not merely prophets and preachers who, conscious of their responsibility for the signs which they use, create their myths to disclose the deeper meaning of the world. It also needs mythologists who critically test these myths to see to what extent they are in harmony with the Christian ethos of truth. In his task the mythologist uses another metalanguage, which again resembles the object-language, albeit on a different level. The object of this language is the mythical language. As we have pointed out elsewhere:

> To put oneself at a distance from the language as "practiced," be it everyday language, scientific language or that of a poet, to question, criticize, correct these languages and, in their place, develop other more precise languages—all this is a function of metalanguage. Any language and any level of language can become the object (the language-object) of a language, of a metalanguage, that is, a language which has another language as the object of its discourse. It goes without saying that theological language in the narrow sense is a meta-language in reference to both the language of proclamation and that

of the magisterium. But is there a metalanguage in reference to the language of theology? Who verifies the statements of theology with respect to the language system? Philosophy? Or contemporary theology in reference to traditional theology? Every discussion and methodological reflection within theology is already a work of metalanguage. What are the characteristics of this metalanguage, what is its method, its terminology? Shouldn't there be a structural analysis of theology? And where would its place be in the system?[4]

If this self-critique of religious language is omitted and if religious language also objects to being questioned from without, then it will inevitably fall victim to the very myths which are its own creation. The structural, to which the mythical statement belongs, then becomes the structurell, the reality intended; and what should be a means to free man then becomes a chain that enslaves him. One then no longer dares to touch the myth, the dogmatic formula, which is man's own creation, because its uncritical use has changed it into the reality itself; all that man is expected to do is simply submit to it. Here lies the cradle of the pseudo-worlds which have brought discredit to religious language in general. Christianity should know that it must constantly demythologize itself and other secondary systems of meaning if it wishes to be taken seriously in matters where of necessity one can speak only mythologically.

2. *Myth, the Reconciliation of Structure and History*

Necessary as the first two reflective and critical attitudes toward the myth are, it would be inhuman to blame man if he

---

4. Günther Schiwy, "Strukturalismus und Theologie," *Theologie und Philosophie*, vol. 43 (1968), pp. 529 f.

also brings about, cultivates and loves the third attitude, which is that of surrendering to the myth. He thereby takes up its truth, he lets the myth play its role in himself in order to have a living contact with its truth. Like any religion, Christianity does not merely tolerate this attitude but considers it a precondition for a deeper penetration into the ultimate dimension of the world and for an objective critique of the myth itself. A mythologist must not primarily pay attention to the dangers which are conjured up by the myth, as Roland Barthes appears to suggest in the above-quoted text. But precisely because he is able to assume the third attitude, the mythologist must also reflectively throw light on the positive aspect of the myth. Lévi-Strauss is an example in this matter.

To preserve the specific characteristics of mythical thinking, he says, we must be able to show that the myth is both the same as language and also different from it. Now *langue* and *parole* are distinguished by the different time referents which they use. But the myth uses a third time referent, which combines the properties of the other two. A myth always refers to events alleged to have happened long ago. But what gives an inner value to the myth is this that the specific pattern of those events is timeless; it explains the past, the present, as well as the future. This double structure—both historical and ahistorical—explains how the myth, while belonging to the realm of the *parole* as well as that of the *langue* in which it is expressed, has also the additional character of an absolute entity on the third level. While this third level is also of a linguistic nature, it is nonetheless different from the other two.

One could describe the myth, Lévi-Strauss adds, as that kind of discourse in which the saying *traduttore traditore* reaches its lowest truth value. In this respect the myth's position on the scale of linguistic expressions lies at the opposite extreme to that of poetry. Poetry is a form of speech which can be translated only with the greatest difficulty and numerous distortions. The value of the myth, on the other hand, is preserved even in the worst translation. The substance of the myth doesn't lie in its style, its rhythm, or its syntax, but in the story it tells. Myth is language functioning on a very high level, where meaning becomes, as it were, detached from its linguistic basis.[5]

Christianity can confirm Lévi-Strauss's remarks from its own self-understanding and the dangers which constantly threaten it. There are historical events to which Christianity attaches structures of salvation history; e.g., the incarnation of God in Jesus of Nazareth. To the extent that these historical events are lost under these structures, the mythological edifice becomes unbalanced. The myth then tends toward speculations having the character of philosophy of religion. From its very inception Christianity was threatened by this danger in gnosticism. Reversely, the Christian myth becomes merely an interesting contribution to the history of religion or the poetic condensation of an individual's lot when the salvation-historical structures recede behind the event. Examples of this tendency can be found in one of the nineteenth century trends of theology. In this respect it is significant that the Bible uses both poetic and speculative language to keep its myth intact. In Christianity

---

5. *Structural Anthropology*, Basic Books, New York, 1963, pp. 209 f.

both these languages are subordinated on the highest level to the mythological system as the reconciliation of event and structure, of history and system.

3. Poetry as Opponent of the Myth

Roland Barthes makes the penetrating remark that precisely in our time poetry is developing into the opponent of the myth, probably as a reaction to the fact that the existing religious systems indulge in a false and twisted mythologization of things and events. He writes as follows:

> Here we have another language which opposes the myth as much as possible, viz., poetic language. Contemporary poetry is a regressive semiological system. While the myth aims at an "ultra meaning," at the enlargement of a primary system, poetry on the contrary, tries to recover an internal meaning, a pre-semiological condition of the language. Poetry tries to change the sign back into its meaning. Its deliberate ideal would be to reach, not the meaning of the words, but the meaning of the things themselves. That's why poetry bewilders the language, increases the abstractness of the concept and the arbitrariness of the sign as much as it can, and loosens the bond between the signifier and the signified to the greatest possible limits. The indeterminate structure of the concept is exploited here to the highest degree. In contrast to prose, the poetic sign tries to make the entire potential of the signified present, in the hope of finally arriving at a kind of transcendent property of the thing, at its natural—that is, not human—meaning. That's why poetry has its essentialistic ambitions, its conviction that it alone can grasp the *matter* itself, precisely insofar as it wishes to be an anti-language. Of all users of words, poets are fundamentally the least formalistic; for they alone think that the

meaning of words is nothing but a form with which they as realists cannot be satisfied. Here lies the reason why our modern poetry shows itself as a murder of language, as a kind of spatial, perceptible analogon with silence. Poetry occupies a position opposite to the myth. The myth is a semiological system which claims to transcend itself in a system of facts; but poetry is a semiological system which claims to reduce itself to an essential system.[6]

To correct Roland Barthes with Lévi-Strauss, even in the Bible poetry does not simply struggle against the myth but against the myth's temptation to philosophize. But aside from this, Christianity throughout its history has always had recourse to poetry. Mystical language is strikingly close to poetry; and the mystics with their language have over and over again brought the language of speculative theology into disarray, thereby liberating it to become itself again. How often also hasn't a self-critical theology used poetic language to reconnect speculation with the living faith. The present crisis of Christianity and its theology is in this respect a thoroughly positive crisis. There is a solid reason for the triumphant feeling with which contemporaries compare abstract theological speculation, so often lost in vagueness and falsehood, to the truth shining forth in the concrete individual. It is all to the good that such things shake the system. And it is no sheer coincidence that even theologians today prefer to write a poetic-sounding essay to a systematic treatise. Christianity is regenerating itself as a mythological system, and in this task modern poetry is its ally.[7]

---

6. *Mythologies*, pp. 234 f.
7. Cf. the author's "Moderne Lyrik und Meditation" *Strukturen christlicher Existenz*, ed by H. Schlier, Würzburg, 1968, pp. 233 ff.

4. *Ideology as Power-supporting Myth*

This structuralistic way of conceiving the myth also throws a new light on ideology. As long as it does not degenerate, the myth created by a society has a thoroughly positive function. But we have to do with an ideology in the structuralistic sense as soon as a society takes possession of the myth to such an extent that it exaggerates its ahistorical element for the purpose of developing a static world-view which will enable this society to proclaim that its structures also are fixed and immutable.

According to Roland Barthes, this tendency is the very "nature" of the myth, but we cannot agree with him. He arrives at this negative view of the myth because he limits his analysis to the contemporary myth in civil society. But he is right when he describes the myth of this society primarily in terms of this function. This is what Roland Barthes says:

> In contemporary bourgeois society, then, the transition from reality to ideology is defined as the transition from *anti-nature* to *pseudo-nature*. Here we find the myth again. Semiology has taught us that it is the task of the myth to establish the historical intention as nature, the contingent as eternity. This is precisely what happens in a bourgeois ideology. If our society is objectively the privileged domain of mythical meaning, the reason is that the myth is formally the most appropriate instrument of ideological reversing; it is defined by it. The myth reverses *antinature* into *pseudonature* on all levels of human communication.
>
> The world provides the myth with an historical reality which is defined . . . by the way people have produced or used it. The myth returns a *natural* picture of this reality. . . . In the myth the memory of how things came about is lost. The world enters language as a dialectical relationship of activities, of human acts; and the world

comes forth from the myth as an harmonious picture of essences. A sleight-of-hand has been worked; reality has been turned over, emptied of history and filled with nature. . . .

Now we are able to complete the semiological definition of the myth in bourgeois society: *the myth is a "depoliticized" statement.* The term "political" should, of course, be understood here as the totality of human relationships in their real, social structure, in their power of producing the world. The prefix *de* in particular should be given an active value; it represents an operative movement, it unceasingly actualizes a loss. For instance, in the case of the Negro soldier the idea that France is an empire is certainly not eliminated; on the contrary, this is precisely what the picture should convey. What is eliminated is the historical, conditioned—in a word, the *fabricated*—quality of colonialism. The myth doesn't deny the facts; its function, on the contrary, consists in speaking of them. But it simply purifies them, makes them innocent, presents them as something natural and eternal; it provides them with a clarity that does not explain but ascertains. When I *ascertain* that France is an empire without explaining this, very little is needed to make me find this condition of being an empire natural and *unquestionable*; and then I am at ease.[8]

5. *"Repoliticizing" Theology*

There cannot be any doubt that Christianity has contributed to the rise of civil society. Influenced by Greek and Roman philosophies, religions and social systems, Christianity put more emphasis on the "mythological" or static element of the myth than on the "mythogenic" or dynamic element which is the original characteristic of Judaism and Christianity.[9] Just as

---

8. *Op. cit.,* pp. 251 f.

9. Cf. the author's essay in *Theologie und Philosophie,* vol. 43 (1968), pp. 531 ff., about these concepts and the "little semantic universe" built of them.

undoubtedly, civil society in its turn has influenced the Christianity of its time. Thus, instead of correcting each other, they strengthened each other in the progressive ideologization of the myth. The result of this is the kind of thinking in terms of a static system which afflicts both these social entities today. It is high time that this fateful symbiosis come to an end, time for Christianity to be mindful of its origin and renew itself in this respect, time to become active as a critical element within the static systems of society, whether they are of a bourgeois or revolutionary origin.

The new theology, which places the concept of salvation history at the center of its attention, seems to have taken this road. And when today there is even talk of "repoliticizing" theology and a "theology of revolution," one can see behind these programs something more than mere attempts to make friends of a theology that tries to sell itself. They are attempts to liberate the Christian myth from its ideological misuse. But care must be taken that in the process this myth is not captured by the opposite ideology and made to serve a revolution which refuses to recognize any lasting identity whatsoever in Christianity.

Perhaps one proceeds too light-heartedly if one gives credit to Christianity for the initiative to change nature emanating from the physical sciences which originated in the West, because Christianity stripped nature of its divinity and placed it at man's disposal. Such a procedure forgets how the Christian myth of creation again condemned this task of man to remain historically inoperative by changing it into the ideology of a statically conceived order of creation, an order entrusted to man for its preservation and not for development. This unfortunate attitude of official Christianity to nature, which still perdures today, delayed the development of the control over nature entrusted to man. Christianity in its ecclesiastical form cannot delude itself into thinking that Western man did not have to secure his role as an extension of the Creator's arm by stubbornly going against Christianity. Perhaps he did this under the impulse of the original spirit of Christianity; but in that case this spirit was then more purely preserved in its secularized form than as systematized and ideologized by the Church.

6. *Power Ideology and Dogmatism*

The discussion occurring today within Christianity and its established social forms, particularly the Catholic Church, make us realize how deeply the need of "civil" man to preserve the status quo at all cost has become ingrained even in the Church. Here again the issue is power structures that are not to be changed because, so it is alleged, they belong to the "nature" of the Church and are even of "divine right." One may not wish to claim that such an argument should *a priori* be opposed. But even then it does not make sense to absolutely reject, in the name of this "myth," any inquiry as to what extent one has to do here with the original Christian myth or with its degeneration into a power ideology. Some protagonists of a statically conceived ecclesiastical establishment disregard in their argumentation precisely the history, the development of this establishment and act as if their concept were given with the nature of the Church and belongs to this "nature." The least one can say about such people is that they appear desirous of changing the myth into ideology.

Another pointer to ideological trends in Christianity is the widespread tendency to state and settle Christian views without explaining them. In defense of this practice, it is said that "faith" is precisely concerned with "inexplicable" matters and that the modern insistence on explanations is a typical manifestation of that "Illumination" which has always unjustifiably importuned Christianity. But such a defense consists of "statements" about "statements"; they may be countered at least in this way: even according to the Christian view, the inexplicable begins only where man's efforts to reach understanding have obviously reached their limits. But I cannot *a priori* determine these limits, I must even fundamentally take into account that there is a possibility of a shift of these limits, for the Christian also has a promise of progress in understanding the faith. There has been much less effort to arrive at an understanding in theology than one would be inclined to think. If theology has been largely disappointing, the reason is not that it has proceeded too scientifically but not scientifically enough. (The term "scientific" should be understood here in the sense that is appropriate to theology.) Theology has too often worked with mere "statements that it is so"; it has systematized them and presented them as "dogmatics," where critical work should have been done precisely on the "dogmatic" composition. Theology must fulfill this function not only in reference to its own statements but also with respect to the magisterium and the practical proclamation of the faith. These uncritical "statements that it is so" are lightheartedly used, and with the same glibness an angry reaction awaits anyone who dares to ask a critical question. While this situation can be understood, it is nonetheless inexcusable. If theology fails to fulfill its task in this matter, it becomes an accomplice in the ideologization of Christianity.

Chapter Eight

SYNCHRONY AND DIACHRONY

THE MATTER TO WHICH THE PAIR of opposite concepts "synchrony" and "diachrony" refers has often already occurred in the preceding chapters. It is time now to consider these concepts explicitly. According to Roland Barthes, this pair is the second important distinction made by French structuralism. He writes as follows:

> One must probably return to pairs of concepts such as *signifier* and *signified*, *synchrony* and *diachrony* to approach that by which structuralism differs from other ways of thinking. The first of these pairs is important because it refers to the linguistic model devised by de Saussure and because linguistics, together with economics, is today *the* science of structure. The second pair is even more important because it obviously entails a certain revision of the concept of history. Although the idea of *synchrony* was for de Saussure mainly an operative concept, this idea conveys a certain standing-still of time; the idea of *diachrony*, on the other hand, is meant to represent the historical process as a mere succession of forms. These two concepts are particularly distinctive because today the main opposition to structuralism really appears to come from the direction of the Marxists and to center on the concept of history and not on that of structure. Be this as it may, ultimately the distinguishing mark of structuralism must probably be seen in the serious attention to the meaning of the

word and not to the word itself, which paradoxically is not at all distinctive. One need to observe only who uses the terms *signifier* and *signified*, *synchrony* and *diachrony* to know whether the structuralistic attitude is present.[1]

Ferdinand de Saussure was successful and became the founder of structural linguistics precisely because in the investigation of language he had the courage to concentrate on its fixed system without denying the development of language. But the tendency to "fix," to answer the question about origins in terms of the system, is an attitude which makes sense only if I abstract from the question about the system's own origin and simply start with the system itself. And this is what the structuralist, as a faithful disciple of de Saussure explicitly does.

Speech, says de Saussure, always implies both an established system and an evolution; at every moment it is an existing institution and a product of the past. At first glance it seems very simple to distinguish between the system and its history, between what it is and what it was. Actually, however, the two are so intimately connected that it is difficult to keep them apart. Would the question be simplified if we studied the linguistic phenomenon in its first stages if e.g. we began by studying the speech of the child? No, for in linguistic matters it is completely misleading to assume that the problem of the first stages differs from that of the permanent conditions. Such an approach offers no escape from the vicious circle. So far de Saussure.[2]

If structuralism is the science of the system's interconnection and if it is necessary to bring time to a standstill in order to be

1. *Essays critiques*, ed. du Seuil, Paris, 1964, pp. 190 f.
2. *Course in General Linguistics*, p. 9.

able to grasp the system as system, there are no objections to this methodic self-restriction. Certain insights of structuralism may be valid at first only for the sign system of language, although even there they continue to be contested; for instance, the idea that the history of language is nothing but the history of forms while their contents remain in principle the same. When such insights are light-heartedly transferred to other systems, including those of the structurell realm, they become questionable. It is also a questionable procedure when the question about the system's origin is not merely declared irrelevant for the structuralist, who makes it a presupposition, but is described as fundamentally unscientific and meaningless. Such trespasses on the part of structuralists must be discussed on the level to which they belong, which is that of philosophy and theology. The first question, however, that must be asked is to what extent the distinction between synchrony and diachrony can be useful for a structural analysis of Christianity.

1. *God's "Surveying Look" as Christian Synchrony*

Let us once again underscore something which we have already stressed on other occasions, viz., how close traditional Christianity is to synchrony. True, Christianity has always been interested in its own origin; it has even explicitly set the time of Jesus apart from the "time before" and the "time of the Church." The formula *Anno Domini* in the Western style of chronology in a general way gives expression to this distinction. This diachronic perspective, however, became, and continued to be, embedded in the typically Christian synchrony, the "surveying look" of God for whom nothing is hidden of all that was, is and will be, who foresees everything from all eternity and who in his revelation has let the Christian share in this "surveying glance." The key figure of world history, then, is Christ; whatever happens must be "read" toward him or from him; the whole of the world is "christologically structured."

On the basis of literary studies and in terms that sound structuralistic, Erich Auerbach offers an excellent description of this Christian attitude toward history:

> The interpretation of the figure "posits a connection between two events or persons in which one of these stands not only for himself or itself but also means the other, while the latter includes or fulfills the former. The two poles of the figure are separated in time but, as real events or persons, they are in time; both are contained in the fleeting stream which life historically is. Only the understanding, the *intellectus spiritualis*, of their interconnection is a spiritual act" (*Figura*, Arch. Roman., 22, 436). In practice it is nearly always a matter of interpreting the Old Testament; its particular events are interpreted as figures or "material" prophecies of the New Testament events. . . .
>
> This kind of interpretation introduces, as one can readily understand, an entirely new and foreign element into the way of looking at ancient history. For example, Isaac's sacrifice is interpreted as a prefiguration of Christ's sacrifice, so that the latter is, as it were, announced and promised in the former; the latter "fulfills" the former, as is expressed by the words *figuram implere*. When such an interpretation is made, a connection is posited between two events which are neither temporally nor causally connected. In the horizontal "run" of time—if we may use this term to indicate a dimension of time—such a connection cannot at all be rationally posited. The interconnection can only be established if one vertically connects both events with God's providence, which alone can plan history in this way and alone can offer the key to knowledge of the interconnection. The horizontal

time connection and the causal connection of events are dissolved; the here and now belongs to an earthly "run"; it is something that has always already been and, at the same time, is something that will be fulfilled in the future. Properly speaking, in "God's sight" it is something eternal, something everlasting, something that has already been accomplished in the fragmentary history of the earth.

This conception of history is endowed with a grandiose unity, but it is also entirely foreign to the mentality of classical antiquity; it upset this mentality even in the very structure of its language. At least its literary language with its ingenious, finely shaded conjunctions, its rich apparatus of syntactical arrangement, its carefully developed chronological system, became wholly superfluous when the earthly relationship of place, time and cause was no longer relevant and a vertical upward connection of all events, converging in God, became the only element of importance. When these two conceptions of history met, it was inevitable that a conflict should arise and attempts to come to an agreement should be made—attempts to reconcile, on the one hand, a conception which carefully interconnected the different parts of history, which observed the order of time and cause and which remained within the realm of the earthly foreground and, on the other hand, a conception which proceeded with abrupt leaps and which everywhere demanded an interpretation from above.[3]

2. *Contemplation and Evolution*

This Christian way of embedding diachrony into synchrony, which in many respects resembles the structuralist's preference for synchrony, is full of dangers. The first of these is the idea that history consists in nothing but different ways of "stating" the one fundamental structure of the world. The world itself knows no development, no progress; whatever progress there

---

3. *Mimesis*, 3rd ed., Bern, 1964, pp. 77 f.

is belongs to the progressive clarification of these structures in man's knowledge. To be man thus does not mean actively to bring the world closer to its goal but meditatively to await its full revelation. Here lies the root of the Western-Christian contemplation: action is made to serve contemplation by opening up to it the "eternal" structures of the world, whenever such a service is necessary.

This attitude has its dangerous consequences for the Christian's involvement in history. The issue is no longer to improve or fundamentally change the structures of the world, to create new structures and to make first a project of the future; no, the important thing is to preserve the structures of the world when they correspond to the fundamental "christological" structure and to see to it that in other respects this fundamental structure prevails and dominates. In line with this conservative tendency there is also a certain vertical individualism and isolationism in the following sense: what is effective and important in history is not so much the causal interconnection of human activities but the care of each individual to be a "figure" of Christ, to do God's will. Everything is all right with the world if everyone, taken individually, is "in order," and this is the case if everyone is an "image" of the God to whose likeness he has been created. The interconnection of history is not so much created by the common action of people as by the essential orientation of all to the same archetype.

Christianity has not always overcome these dangers. Its relationship to history has not always been one of balance between synchrony and diachrony. Yet its task is precisely to preserve such a balance. For God did not reveal himself in Christ as the

static foundation of a world in whose structures man has merely to find his place, but as the dynamic principle of the world's
development: everything has been created in Christ to find its
consummate form through him, by letting Christ grow in itself.
The divine structuring of the world is itself a process, it is God's
becoming world and man which is accomplished in the course
of mankind's history. This process, however, has its phases, its
stages of development and of setbacks, for it is a struggle of
God with man's freedom, the freedom through which the process
takes place. Here lies the source from which this history gets
its distinctive features, its structural differences; here lies the
reason why every individual situation is something serious and
why every individual is responsible for the whole. For everything is connected with everything else, not only in the figure
but also causally.

The reproach Sartre addresses to the structuralists can also
be applied to Christians who would rather let the so-called
"saved world" carry them forward toward their destiny than
commit themselves to develop "saving" structures in the world.
Sartre says:

> You remember Auguste Comte's words: "Progress is the develop-
> ment of order." This is precisely the way the structuralists conceive
> diachrony: man evolves, so to speak, through the evolution of the
> structures. I don't think that history can be reduced to this inner pro-
> cess. History is not order but disorder, let us say, it is a rational dis-
> order. Precisely at the moment when history keeps the order, i.e., the
> structure, standing, it also begins again to dissolve this order. . . .
>
> Althusser claims that man makes history without realizing it; he
> holds that it is not history which lays claim to man but it is the struc-
> tural totality in which he is situated that conditions him. History is

engulfed in the structures. But Althusser disregards that there is a constant contradiction between the practico-inert structure and the man who discovers that he is conditioned by this structure. Each generation distances itself from these structures in a different way, and this is what makes the change of the structures possible.[4]

3. *Resignation and Freedom or "Dialogue with a Cat"*

Sartre's critique puts the Marxist Althusser in a strange kind of twilight: after the most recent experiences with Marxism, can a neo-Marxist still remain so well-disposed toward the system? But Sartre's critique also makes the Christian ask whether an exaggerated synchrony does not lead to a psychological association which easily terminates in social totalitarianism or in fatalistic nihilism. Both these tendencies can be observed among structuralists who make of the diachrony a moment of the synchrony which is constantly being swallowed up by the latter.

The texts quoted at the beginning of this book in the "short history of structuralism" can serve to illustrate the relativizing, dehumanizing and nihilistic tendency. The structuralism which is socially conservative and politically supports the established system, and which thereby itself becomes an ideology, cannot as readily be illustrated; yet this doesn't allow one to say that it does not exist and is a "myth." The biography of many structuralists goes from political involvement to contemplative structuralism, and this is no coincidence. And the "structurell-functional theory" of positivistic sociologists and political scientists does not seem to be far removed from the above-men-

---

4. "Jean-Paul Sartre Répond," *L'Arc*, no. 30, 1966, pp. 90, 93.

tioned ideology.[5] There is no escape from the system; it is the stronger element, and every change of systems is merely a "matter of form" in the most literal sense of the term, a new combination of always the same elements. Revolution doesn't pay, and the only true revolution is man's growing realization that the system is devoid of prospects. Lévi-Strauss writes:

> The world started without man and will end without him. The institutions, morals and customs which throughout my life I have tried to list and understand are the perishable flowering of a creation in relation to which they have no meaning, except perhaps that of permitting mankind to play its role in this creation. But this role doesn't give man an independent position; his vain endeavor consists in a useless struggle against universal decay; man himself appears as a machine. . . . When one day the rainbow of man's civilizations will have vanished into the abyss dug by our fury, there will still be, as long as we and as long as the world exists, that slender "bow" which connects us with the inaccessible. This "bow" shows us that road which we haven't followed, the road which would have led us out of slavery, and the contemplation of which gives man the only grace for which he should strive, viz., the grace to interrupt the march, to tame the impulse which compels him to fill, one by one, the open fissures in the wall of necessity and thus to complete his work at the very moment when he has built his prison.
>
> This is the grace desired by every society, whatever its religious convictions, its political system and culture may be. It is in this grace that any society finds its leisure, its delight, its rest and its freedom. It is that vital power by which, in the brief moments when the human condition tolerates it, it can interrupt its bee-like activity, seize the essence of what it has been and still is, go beyond thinking and beyond society to contemplate a mineral more beautiful than all man-made things, inhale the fragrance of a lily-cup, wiser than our books,

5.   Cf. Schiwy, *Der französische Strukturalismus*, pp. 29 f., 86-98.

and hold a dialogue with a cat in all patience, seriousness and mutual indulgence.[6]

No matter how contemplative and "resigned to God's will" all this sounds, it has nothing in common with Christianity. But it is the ultimate consequence of dispositions found in traditional Christianity. The attitude to which they lead among structuralists should make Christians self-critical with respect to similar temptations which they may face. The slogans, "Peace at any price" and "No criticism for peace's sake," should find no adherents in Christianity. A smoothly functioning system, as peaceful as a cemetery, can never be a Christian system, for Christianity wishes man to be alive and grow ever more in freedom and truth. In this respect freedom is the pre-condition of self-determination and something that must be respected by all.

When a Christian Church as an organized system takes "care" of the individual in such a total way that his development is restricted or even prevented, it becomes a totalitarian system, and this is something which is essentially unchristian. That such a situation is not merely a theoretical possibility for Christians is evident from a look at Church history, particularly the development of certain Christian sects and States. Human freedom constantly puts the system into question, not in a fundamental way but by asking whether the system retains its serving function. That's why systems which do not wish to run the risk involved in man's freedom are inclined to do away with the subject in a theoretical-structuralistic way and to oppress him in practice. In the struggle between the forces of history

6. *Tristes tropiques*, pp. 447 ff.

demanding development with conservative systems averse to change, a Church may attempt to solve the problem of synchrony and diachrony by onesidedly favoring the conservative forces. But even if a Church merely seems to do this, it makes Christianity incredible, it demolishes belief that freedom, personality and progress are possible in it and thus it ruins itself.

Lévi-Strauss consoles himself with the idea that in his prison man can always engage in a "dialogue with a cat." The Christian Teilhard de Chardin, who has investigated the world just as much as his structuralistic colleague, did not despise the "dialogue with a cat," but he "saw" even in this dialogue that our system is not a prison but openness. Wherever systems are closed, whether in the Church or outside it, whether in the West or the East, human beings are responsible for this, and they should be called to account. But this idea presupposes that one believes in the possibility of freedom because one has already seen and experienced its reality now and then. The Christian believes that in Christ he has seen with all clarity what one can already suspect in the "dialogue with a cat":

> In the behavior of a cat, a dog, a dolphin, what a flexibility! . . . How great the role played by the love of life and curiosity! Instinct is here no longer narrowly channeled and immobilized to a single function, as it is for a spider or a bee. In the individual animal as well as in the group it remains pliant. It is interested, it toys, it enjoys. . . . Unlike the insect, the mammal is no longer a slavishly dependent member of the phylum with which it made its appearance. An "aura" of freedom begins to surround it, there is a first faint glimmer of personality.[7]

---

7. Quoted after Johannes Hemleben, *Teilhard de Chardin*, Rororo monograph, p. 131.

INDEX OF NAMES

103

INDEX OF SUBJECT MATTER